CAKES THAT WOW COOKBOOK

CAKES THAT WOW COOKBOOK

A Beginner's Guide to Baking
and Decorating Spectacular Cakes

Christina Wu
(aka Bake-a-Saurus)

ROCKRIDGE
PRESS

Interior and Cover Designer: Jami Spittler
Art Producer: Sara Feinstein
Editor: Anne Lowrey
Production Editor: Jax Berman
Production Manager: Martin Worthington

Cover photography © 2022 Elysa Weitala. Cover food styling by Victoria Woollard. Interior photography © 2022 Christina Wu. Illustration used under license from Shutterstock.

Paperback ISBN: 978-1-63878-603-0
eBook ISBN: 978-1-63807-699-5
R0

CONTENTS

INTRODUCTION

CAKE IS MY LOVE LANGUAGE. Baking flavorful layers and wrapping them up in delicious buttercream is my form of poetry. I look forward to being a part of a couple's special day, a friend's birthday, or a family member's graduation by bringing something everyone can enjoy. To me, cake is more than just a dessert at the end of a meal. It signifies celebration and joy and helps create wonderful memories.

Until about five years ago, my experience with cakes was limited to reading the instructions off a box and making a simple whipped cream. After my partner and I moved to a new city, I began to experiment with other baked goods. The addition of a stand mixer to our new kitchen made for a notable turning point. I started with cookies and brownies and branched out to croissants and macarons.

At the same time, I started sharing my baking journey on social media. It was then that I came across a wonderful community full of fellow hobby bakers. Part of this baking community was a myriad of cake artists whose work caught my eye. I admired how they took layers of cake and turned them into beautiful works of art. I started to watch videos and tutorials from a wide range of decorators and began practicing on my own. I often refer to this period of introduction to decorating as a rabbit hole of learning. I had plenty of failures and mishaps; it was not easy and perfect from the get-go. But I really loved it, more than any other hobby I have picked up. I kept at it and eventually found my comfort zone as a buttercream decorator.

I started from the very basics: baking sheet cakes and learning how to pair them with buttercream. From there, I learned about stacking and filling layered and tiered cakes. I also discovered I quite enjoyed making beautiful cupcakes and other cake-filled treats and am excited to share those creations with you. All the while you will be picking up helpful baking skills and using them to cultivate your cake-decorating skills.

In this book, you will learn how to take the basic foundations of baking cakes and turn them into sweets that tell stories. I will cover everything from the equipment necessary to have a successful baking venture to decorating cakes in a fun and creative fashion. This includes the basic steps in between, such as leveling layers, achieving smooth cake sides, and working with pastry bags and piping tips. I have also included some of my go-to recipes for baking basic cakes that will help get even the most beginner-level decorator started.

I hope you experience learning about decorating the way I did: as a fun outlet for creativity. You will find your own style and learn various techniques along the way. Your cakes will be unique to you and will take on a signature style. Whether you are running a small bakery or simply looking for an enjoyable new hobby, this guide is perfect for starting from scratch. For me, the best part is always learning something new, and I continue to develop new skills as a cake maker every time I enter the kitchen.

So, gather up your baking tools, put on an apron, and get out your sprinkle collection (if you don't have one, you will very soon!). Try out the recipes and tutorials that appeal to you the most, and explore your creativity with your cakes each time you practice.

YOUR CAKE KITCHEN

Before getting started, you will want to ensure you have the equipment necessary for a successful baking venture. I've listed the necessary bakeware, such as cake pans and spatulas, and you will also learn about tools needed to decorate cakes. We will go over scrapers, palette knives, and some other fun tools that will help you get creative with your cakes. We will also devote some time to learning about types of food coloring and the various methods for using them. By the end of this chapter, you should have a good idea of what to prepare your kitchen with to produce beautiful cakes.

···EQUIPMENT···

If you are just starting out and learning how to bake, you may want to purchase affordable, basic equipment and later down the line decide to invest in some long-lasting bakeware. I will briefly discuss some standard cake pan sizes that are also necessary for the recipes found in this book. Then, you will learn about the essential pieces of equipment that can be of great assistance for baking and decorating. This includes mixers, sifters, and mixing bowls. Finally, you will get to explore supplies that will help you create unique cake designs, such as textured combs and silicone molds.

Cake Pans

For decorating tall and large cakes, I tend to use my 6-inch or 9-inch round pans. For adding a small tier to a multilevel cake, I use a 4-inch round pan. And for the sheet cake recipes that you will find later in the book, you will need a 9-by-13-inch aluminum or glass pan.

9-inch round pan: I use this size for the supporting tier of multitiered cakes and for large party cakes.

6-inch round pans: For the recipes in this book, you will need four of these. They help create the tall double-barrel look.

4-inch round pans: You can also use a silicone cavity mold that can be purchased from most online retailers.

9-inch-by-13-inch sheet cake pan: You can find these in either aluminum or glass, and they are great for basic sheet cakes like the ones in chapter 4.

To make multiple layered 9-by-13-inch sheet cakes, aluminum pans are recommended.

Must-Have Tools and Supplies

Consider these your essential pieces of equipment for baking cakes. I use every one of these items when preparing cake layers and while decorating. They are easily purchased from many online retailers.

Electric hand mixer or stand mixer: Having a reliable mixer with a whisk attachment is standard for most buttercream, meringue-based, and whipping cream recipes.

Large mixing bowls: You will need large bowls for making cake batter. I have an assortment of sizes, all of which have different uses.

Rubber/silicone spatulas: Scrape down mixing bowls to get the most out of the ingredients. Use them for mixing colors and various edible mediums.

Whisk: Most of the recipes in this book require a large whisk for mixing cake batter.

Cake boards/drums: You will need a base to decorate your cakes on. While cardboard ones are cheap and always available, I suggest investing in some acrylic ones or the wrapped kinds known as drums.

Cake leveler: There are some great quality cake levelers out here, but a simple and affordable wire one like the one shown in the second image above will get the job done for trimming flat surfaces on cake layers.

Cake scraper/smoother: These can be metal, acrylic, or plastic. They're great for getting nice smooth cake sides (affectionately called "bellies" in the cake decorating world).

Flour sifter: Sifting is an important step for avoiding large lumps of flour in the batter.

Kitchen scale: While the recipes in this book call for measurements in imperial units, you may also come across recipes that use metric units. For this, a digital scale is handy for weighing out in grams.

Nonslip mat: Your cake will go flying off the turntable without one of these. I'm serious.

Oven thermometer: Ovens vary widely, and temperature readings are not always reliable. Use an oven thermometer to get a more accurate reading.

Palette knife: These are handy when smoothing down and leveling the top of a cake. They are slightly angled so that your wrist is at a comfortable degree to create a flat surface.

Pastry brush: I typically brush over my cake layers right out of the oven with a simple syrup or milk mixture to keep them moist.

Turntable: This is arguably your most important decorating tool; I've used it for every cake I have made for the past three years.

Nice-to-Have Tools and Supplies

In addition to fundamental tools, there are tools that are best to keep around for increasingly complex and beautiful designs. As soon as you are comfortable with your basic cake-decorating skills, explore some of these fun additions to your kitchen repertoire.

Acrylic cake discs: Some decorators prefer to use these as guides for scraping smooth and even sides.

Cake brushes: From fine to fluffy, brushes are great for fine details and covering large areas.

Cake strips: Using cloth strips specially fit for covering the sides of pans will help avoid some of the caramelization that occurs on the sides of cakes, as well as help bake a flat and even cake.

Cupcake corers: Remove the middle portion of the cupcake so that you can fill it with something yummy.

Fondant roller: Smooth and roll out fondant for covering cake and other decorative elements.

Fondant tools: To achieve small details, various shaped tools can help carry fondant work a long way.

Piping bags: Tips and bags go hand in hand. I included these items in the nice-to-have list because it is entirely possible to decorate a cake without them. It's a matter of personal preference.

Piping tips: There are a wide variety of piping tips out there perfect for people who enjoy piping borders and other details onto their cakes.

Silicone baking mat: These are great to use when working with fondant. I like to use them when working with food coloring as well.

Squeeze bottles: These are perfect for getting nice even drips on a cake if you want something with a little more control than the spoon method.

Tools That Make Cake Decorating Fun

There seems to be an endless array of tools that make decorating extra fun. There are various molds, brushes, cutters, stamps, rollers, and many more that could take up a whole other book. These are some of my favorites.

Cakesicle/cake pop molds: You can find all sorts of fun shapes for cake pops online, plus cute sticks to go with them.

Cookie cutters: While you may also use them for cookies, cutters have a wide range of uses from fondant cutouts to creating an outline for sprinkle placement.

Edible luster dusts and glitters: These make baked goods shiny, sparkly, and noticeable.

Edible markers/pens: These enable you to add quick details in a wide array of colors.

Lettering sets: These are fun for using on fondant or buttercream and give cakes a nice professional-looking touch.

Silicone shape molds: Sharks, flowers, bees, ghosts, you name it: there's probably a mold out there for anything you search for.

Sprinkles: I may be a little biased, but there's something about sprinkles that really makes a cake super happy.

Stencils: Add an artsy touch with a wide variety of patterns and designs.

Textured/striped combs: These are handy for making bold lines on cakes and highlighting different kinds of textures (scalloped, ridged, etc.).

Tweezers: For fixing those tiny little mistakes and for sprinkle placement (the best part).

• • • FOOD COLORING • • •

Coloring buttercream should be a fun and experimental experience. You may discover which colors you most favor and what you can combine to achieve them. Color mixing has endless possibility!

I love creating a simple palette and letting it blossom into something unique for the cake. I also really enjoy starting with a bit of one color and mixing in another. Let's look at some of the ways you can color not only buttercream but also fondant, ganache, and cakes.

Types of Coloring

There are many types of food coloring that cater to different properties, depending on the edible medium you choose. For instance, gel colors work well with buttercreams but are not ideal for working with chocolate because they cause seizing. A better alternative to coloring chocolate would be oil-based colors. Here are the color types to know about:

Gel colors: Gels have a corn syrup/glycerin base and are more concentrated than liquid colors. These are great for achieving intense colors.

Liquid colors: These are water-based and used for a wide variety of things, including coloring dough and cake batter.

Oil-based colors: These are the best kinds to work with chocolates or candy melts, because these types of mediums are oil-based as well.

Powder colors: As the name suggests, powders do not contain any liquid properties. You can mix them with alcohol to get a liquid color or use them dry in something like fondant.

Spray colors: The most popular types are found in aerosol cans and are used to mist over parts of the cake. They primarily contain the same ingredients as liquid food coloring.

Adding Color to Frosting

Color is subjective to the kind of look you want the buttercream to have. Except for the spray color, most options are suitable for buttercream. Oil-based and gel colors work the best for achieving bold shades, while powders are helpful for creating pastels and neutrals. Start by adding a very minimal amount to the buttercream; it is always easier to add color for intensity than it is to take it away. There is also a tempering method, which requires heating up a small amount of the buttercream (just enough to add color) and mixing the coloring into the heated buttercream before adding it to the rest of the frosting.

Adding Color to Fondant

While there are many types of colored fondant available, you may be interested in creating a uniquely colored fondant. Powder and gel colors work the best with fondant, because they do not add moisture, which will make the fondant too sticky to work with. While wearing gloves, work a small amount of color into the fondant by folding it over itself and stretching it out, in a motion similar to pulling taffy. You will also want some confectioners' sugar or cornstarch handy in case the fondant starts to stick. It takes a couple of minutes to work the color in and make sure that it is uniform.

Adding Color to White Chocolate Ganache

For a colorful drip on a cake, you will want to make a ganache recipe like the one for the Chai Chic (page 111) cake. Because ganache is the product of ingredients with high fat contents (cream and chocolate), you will want to use an oil-based color. Oil-based colors bond well with the ganache and help discourage seizing, which is when the ganache starts to solidify due to the addition of moisture (from gel or liquid coloring). To color ganache, add a few drops of the oil-based color and stir slowly until it is incorporated and mixed evenly throughout.

Adding Color to Cakes

Most cake batter can be dyed easily with gel or liquid colors. Either can be used interchangeably to make cakes look colorful and vibrant. I am generous with colors when coloring cake batter, because the intensity tends to weaken while baking. Right after you have mixed in the dry ingredients, add a few drops to see if you are happy with the color. If you are looking for strong, bold cake layers, add extra coloring. Don't be discouraged by the caramelization on top of the cake after it is done baking: leveling or torting will reveal a colorful crumb.

Baking layers for special cakes is part of the fun of decorating. I have included some elementary recipes to get you started on baking those delicious cake layers from scratch and making the frostings that hold them together and make them stand out. You'll also be able to find gluten-free and vegan options for those with dietary restrictions.

After you gain some experience with baking, you will be able to create your own flavor profiles and play with different pairings of buttercream and cake.

YOUR BUILDING BLOCKS:
Cakes and Frostings

BEST-EVER VANILLA CAKE MIX CAKE

EQUIPMENT NEEDED
2 (9-inch) round pans or
  3 (6-inch) round pans

PREP TIME 5 minutes
BAKE TIME 20 to
  25 minutes

MAKES 2 (9-inch) rounds
  or 3 (6-inch) rounds
SERVES 8 to 10

Using a doctored cake mix is popular with bakers of all skill levels. It cuts down on preparation time while still resulting in a delicious cake. This souped-up recipe will produce a fluffy cake with rich vanilla flavor. You will still be using the ingredients listed on the back of the box while making a few substitutions and additions. These doctored cakes are perfect for a party on the whim and can easily be paired with the buttercream recipes found later in this chapter. Personally, I love classic vanilla and make this doctored cake with vanilla buttercream all the time.

FOR THE CAKE
Nonstick baking spray
1 (15.25-ounce) box store-bought
  white cake mix, plus the ingredients
  listed on the back of the box (oil,
  eggs, and replace the water with
  1¼ cups whole milk, at room
  temperature)

½ cup cake flour, sifted
¼ teaspoon baking soda
4 tablespoons (½ stick) salted
  butter, melted
½ cup granulated sugar
½ teaspoon vanilla extract

FOR THE SIMPLE SYRUP
¼ cup water or milk

¼ cup granulated sugar

1. Preheat the oven to 350°F. Spray the pans with baking spray and set aside.

2. In a large bowl, whisk together the cake mix, cake flour, and baking soda. Set aside.

3. In another large bowl, combine the butter, oil, and sugar.

4. Add the eggs one at a time, then the vanilla, and whisk well for about 30 seconds.

5. Add half of the milk and whisk until combined.

6. Sift in half of the dry ingredients and mix well. Add in the rest of the milk, combine, then add the rest of the dry ingredients. Whisk for about 1 minute.

7. Divide the mixture evenly into the prepared pans.

8. Bake for 20 to 25 minutes if you are using the 9-inch rounds and 23 to 28 minutes for the 6-inch rounds, or until a toothpick inserted into the center comes out clean.

9. While the cake is baking, make the simple syrup: In a small saucepan over low heat, combine the water and sugar and mix until the sugar is dissolved. Cool before using (leftovers may be refrigerated).

10. When the cakes are cool enough to handle, remove the cakes from the pans, level, brush with the simple syrup, tort, and chill before decorating.

For detailed explanations of the leveling and torting processes, check out pages 40-41.

Brushing cakes with simple syrup after leveling is an optional but recommended step that helps lock in moisture. Use equal amounts of water mixed with dissolved sugar and brush over the leveled cakes while still warm.

FROM-SCRATCH VANILLA CAKE

EQUIPMENT NEEDED
2 (9-inch) round pans or
  4 (6-inch) round pans

PREP TIME 10 minutes
BAKE TIME 20 to
  25 minutes

MAKES 2 (9-inch) rounds
  or 4 (6-inch) rounds
SERVES 10 to 15

This is a versatile cake that is fun to customize. It can withstand many substitutions (for example, using four egg whites instead of three whole eggs, or replacing the yogurt with sour cream). You can replace the vanilla with any flavoring or extract of choice. The only thing I advise not changing are the dry ingredients. If you go with pure vanilla, this cake has warm notes that pair well with most buttercream flavors.

Nonstick baking spray
2½ cups all-purpose flour
1 teaspoon baking powder
1½ teaspoons baking soda
½ teaspoon salt
8 tablespoons (1 stick) salted butter, at room temperature
½ cup vegetable oil

2 cups granulated sugar
3 large eggs, at room temperature
1 cup plain full-fat yogurt, at room temperature
2 teaspoons vanilla extract
1 cup whole milk, at room temperature, divided
Simple syrup (pages 12–13) (optional)

1. Preheat the oven to 350°F. Spray the pans with baking spray and set aside.

2. In a large bowl, combine the flour, baking powder, baking soda, and salt and whisk together. Set aside.

3. Using a hand mixer or paddle on a stand mixer, cream together the butter, oil, and sugar.

4. Add the eggs one at a time, mixing between each addition.

5. Mix in the yogurt first, then the vanilla, followed by ½ cup of milk.

6. Sift half of the dry ingredients into the wet mixture and whisk well for about 30 seconds.

7. Add the remaining ½ cup of milk and the remainder of the dry ingredients.

8. Use a rubber spatula to scrape down the sides of the bowl and ensure all ingredients are mixed.

9. Mix the batter for 1 to 2 minutes. Try not to overmix.

10. Divid e the batter evenly into the prepared pans.

11. Bake for 20 minutes for the 9-inch rounds and 25 minutes for the 6-inch rounds.

12. Lower the temperature to 325°F and bake an additional 5 minutes. Check with a toothpick to see if it comes out clean, and bake in increments of 2 to 3 minutes if needed.

13. When cool enough to handle, remove the cakes from the pans, level, brush with the simple syrup (if using), tort, and chill before decorating.

BEST-EVER CHOCOLATE CAKE MIX CAKE

EQUIPMENT NEEDED
2 (9-inch) round pans or
  3 (6-inch) round pans

PREP TIME 5 minutes
BAKE TIME 20 to
  25 minutes

MAKES 2 (9-inch) rounds
  or 3 (6-inch) rounds
SERVES 8 to 10

This fluffed-up chocolate recipe is one of the best when it comes to adding a little extra love to a store-bought mix. Any devil's food chocolate cake box mix will work great with these extra ingredients. Add your favorite chocolate buttercream or ganache and you have yourself a bakery-style piece of chocolate cake heaven. This recipe adds even more chocolate flavor and results in a fluffy, moist crumb that is as delicious as a true made-from-scratch recipe.

Nonstick baking spray
1 box store-bought devil's food cake
  mix, plus the ingredients listed on
  the back of the box (oil, eggs, and
  replace the water with 1¼ cups
  whole milk, at room temperature)
½ cup cake flour

¼ cup dark cocoa powder
¼ teaspoon baking soda
4 tablespoons (½ stick) salted
  butter, melted
½ cup granulated sugar
Simple syrup (pages 12–13) (optional)

1. Preheat the oven to 350°F. Spray the pans with baking spray and set aside.

2. In a large bowl, whisk together the cake mix, cake flour, cocoa powder, and baking soda. Set aside.

3. In another large bowl, combine the butter, oil, and sugar.

4. Add the eggs one at a time and whisk well for about 30 seconds.

5. Add half of the milk and whisk until combined.

6. Sift in half of the dry ingredients and mix well. Add in the rest of the milk, combine, then add the rest of the dry ingredients. Whisk for about 1 minute.

7. Divide evenly into prepared pans. Bake for 20 to 25 minutes if you are using the 9-inch rounds and 23 to 28 minutes for the 6-inch rounds, or until a toothpick inserted into the center comes out clean.

8. When cool enough to handle, remove the cakes from the pans, level, brush with the simple syrup (if using), tort, and chill before decorating.

FROM-SCRATCH CHOCOLATE CAKE

EQUIPMENT NEEDED
2 (9-inch) round pans or
  4 (6-inch) round pans

PREP TIME 10 minutes
BAKE TIME 25 to
  30 minutes

MAKES 2 (9-inch) rounds
  or 4 (6-inch) rounds
SERVES 10 to 15

This is arguably my favorite chocolate cake recipe ever. It is not lacking in intense chocolate flavor as it uses cocoa powder as its base. The hint of coffee also helps bring out the chocolate flavor without being overpowering. You don't have to use a dark cocoa powder, but a Dutch-processed or special dark makes all the difference. For the ultimate chocolate experience, pair this with a rich chocolate buttercream or ganache. I also love using fresh berry sauces with this cake, because the sweetness of the berries complements the chocolate flavor so well.

Nonstick baking spray
2½ cups all-purpose flour
¾ cup dark cocoa powder
1½ teaspoons baking powder
1 teaspoon baking soda
½ teaspoon salt
8 tablespoons (1 stick) salted butter, at
  room temperature
½ cup vegetable oil

2 cups granulated sugar
3 large eggs, at room temperature
2 teaspoons espresso powder
1 tablespoon hot water
1 cup plain full-fat yogurt, at room
  temperature
1 cup whole milk, at room
  temperature, divided
Simple syrup (pages 12–13) (optional)

1. Preheat the oven to 350°F. Spray the pans with baking spray and set aside.

2. In a large bowl, combine the flour, cocoa powder, baking powder, baking soda, and salt and whisk together. Set aside.

3. Using a hand mixer or paddle on a stand mixer, cream together the butter, oil, and sugar.

4. Add the eggs one at a time, mixing between each addition.

5. Dissolve the espresso powder in the hot water. Add it to the wet batter.

6. Mix in the yogurt first, followed by ½ cup of milk.

7. Sift half of the dry ingredients into the wet mixture and whisk well for about 30 seconds.

8. Add in the remaining ½ cup of milk and the remainder of the dry ingredients.

9. Use a rubber spatula to scrape down the sides of the bowl and ensure all ingredients are mixed.

10. Mix the batter for 1 to 2 minutes. Try not to overmix.

11. Divide the batter evenly into the prepared pans.

12. Bake for 24 to 27 minutes for the 9-inch rounds and 25 to 30 minutes for the 6-inch rounds, or until a toothpick inserted into the center comes out clean.

13. When cool enough to handle, remove the cakes from the pans, level, brush with the simple syrup (if using), tort, and chill before decorating.

GLUTEN-FREE VANILLA CAKE

EQUIPMENT NEEDED
2 (9-inch) round pans or
   3 (6-inch) round pans

PREP TIME 10 minutes
BAKE TIME 20 to
   25 minutes

MAKES 2 (9-inch) rounds
   or 3 (6-inch) rounds
SERVES 8 to10

As a home baker, I come across orders that request dietary restrictions. One of my most common requests is for gluten-free cakes. After testing many recipes, I was able to develop a rich-tasting vanilla cake that is still fluffy and spongy in texture. For this recipe, I used Bob's Red Mill Gluten-Free 1-to-1 Baking Flour. Out of all the other gluten-free flour options I've tried, this one seems to be the best for this particular cake. It goes well with any buttercream flavor of your choice, especially one that has notes of citrus and berry.

Nonstick baking spray
1¾ cups gluten-free 1:1 flour
1 teaspoon baking soda
½ teaspoon baking powder
½ teaspoon salt
½ cup vegetable oil
4 tablespoons (½ stick) salted
   butter, melted

1¼ cups granulated sugar
2 large eggs, at room temperature
1½ teaspoons vanilla extract
¼ cup plain full-fat yogurt, at room
   temperature
¾ cup whole milk, at room
   temperature
Simple syrup (pages 12–13) (optional)

1. Preheat the oven to 350°F. Spray the pans with baking spray and line the bottoms with a circle of parchment paper. Set aside.

2. In a large bowl, combine the flour, baking soda, baking powder, and salt and whisk together. Set aside.

3. In another large bowl, whisk the oil, butter, and sugar together.

4. Add the eggs one at a time, mixing between each addition. Mix in the vanilla.

5. Mix in the yogurt first, followed by half of the milk.

6. Sift half of the dry ingredients into the wet mixture and whisk well for about 30 seconds.

7. Add in the rest of the milk and the remainder of the dry ingredients.

8. Use a rubber spatula to scrape down the sides of the bowl.

9. Mix the batter for 1 to 2 minutes. The batter should be a tad runny.

10. Divide the batter evenly into the prepared pans.

11. Bake for 18 to 22 minutes for the 9-inch rounds and 24 to 28 minutes for the 6-inch rounds, or until a toothpick inserted into the center comes out clean.

12. When cool enough to handle, remove the cakes from the pans, level, brush with the simple syrup (if using), tort, and chill before decorating.

GLUTEN-FREE CHOCOLATE CAKE

EQUIPMENT NEEDED
2 (9-inch) round pans or 3 (6-inch) round pans

PREP TIME 10 minutes
BAKE TIME 20 to 25 minutes

MAKES 2 (9-inch) rounds or 3 (6-inch) rounds
SERVES 8 to 10

Making a gluten-free cake that is moist and fluffy can be tricky. Using a flour substitute can often lead to dry, tasteless cakes that hardly have any volume. By using a 1:1 gluten-free flour and some standard wet ingredients to mimic the binding nature of regular flour, I was able to develop this rich chocolate cake recipe that is perfect for those with gluten-free restrictions. Pairing it with fresh berries and a velvety chocolate buttercream heightens the decadent flavor, and your guests will find it hard to believe it's gluten-free!

Nonstick baking spray
1½ cups gluten-free 1:1 flour
½ cup dark cocoa powder
1 teaspoon baking soda
½ teaspoon baking powder
½ teaspoon salt
¾ cup vegetable oil
4 tablespoons (½ stick) salted butter, melted

1 cup granulated sugar
2 large eggs, at room temperature
½ teaspoon espresso powder
1 teaspoon hot water
¼ cup plain full-fat yogurt, at room temperature
¾ cup whole milk, at room temperature
Simple syrup (pages 12–13) (optional)

1. Preheat the oven to 350°F. Spray the pans with baking spray and line the bottoms with a circle of parchment paper. Set aside.

2. In a large bowl, combine the flour, cocoa powder, baking soda, baking powder, and salt and whisk together. Set aside.

3. In another large bowl, whisk the oil, butter, and sugar together.

4. Add the eggs one at a time, mixing between each addition.

5. Dissolve the espresso powder in the hot water and add it to the wet mixture.

6. Add in the yogurt and then half of the milk.

7. Sift half of the dry ingredients into the wet mixture and whisk well for about 30 seconds.

8. Add in the rest of the milk and the remainder of the dry ingredients.

9. Use a rubber spatula to scrape down the sides of the bowl.

10. Mix the batter for 1 to 2 minutes. It's okay if the batter is a little runny.

11. Divide the batter evenly into the prepared pans.

12. Bake for 20 to 22 minutes for the 9-inch rounds and 25 to 30 minutes for the 6-inch rounds, or until a toothpick inserted into the center comes out clean.

13. When cool enough to handle, remove the cakes from the pans, level, brush with the simple syrup (if using), tort, and chill before decorating.

VEGAN VANILLA CAKE

EQUIPMENT NEEDED
2 (9-inch) round pans or
  3 (6-inch) round pans

PREP TIME 10 minutes
BAKE TIME 20 to
  25 minutes

MAKES 2 (9-inch) rounds
  or 3 (6-inch) rounds
SERVES 4 to 6

Since this is a smaller cake, you may want to double this recipe and use 4 (6-inch) rounds or 3 (9-inch) rounds. For the yogurt, I use a coconut alternative, and for the milk, I recommend using almond or soy as they are richer than rice or other plant-based milks. My vegan friends have commented on how great of a substitute this is for a classic vanilla cake! It has all the wonderful rich vanilla notes, and the dairy substitutes are hardly noticeable. With this recipe, you won't have to be intimidated by special requests for dairy-free cakes!

Nonstick baking spray
1 cup plant-based milk, at room
  temperature
1 teaspoon apple cider vinegar
1½ cups all-purpose flour
1½ teaspoons baking soda
½ teaspoon baking powder

½ teaspoon salt
1¼ cups granulated sugar
¾ cup vegetable oil
½ cup vanilla or plain plant-based
  yogurt, at room temperature
2 teaspoons vanilla extract
Simple syrup (pages 12–13) (optional)

1. Preheat the oven to 350°F. Spray the pans with baking spray and set aside.

2. In a large bowl or measuring cup, combine the plant-based milk with the vinegar. Give it a good stir and then set aside.

3. In a large bowl, combine the flour, baking soda, baking powder, and salt and whisk together. Set aside.

4. In another large bowl, whisk the sugar and oil together. Add in the yogurt and vanilla. Combine well.

5. Add ½ cup of the milk mixture and whisk for about 10 seconds.

6. Sift half of the dry ingredients into the wet mixture and whisk well for about 15 seconds.

7. Add in the rest of the milk mixture and dry ingredients. Use a rubber spatula to scrape down the sides of the bowl. Mix the batter for about 1 minute.

8. Divide the batter evenly into the prepared pans.

9. Bake for 20 to 22 minutes for the 9-inch rounds and 22 to 26 minutes for the 6-inch rounds, or until a toothpick inserted into the center comes out clean.

10. When cool enough to handle, remove the cakes from the pans, level, brush with the simple syrup (if using), tort, and chill before decorating.

VEGAN CHOCOLATE CAKE

EQUIPMENT NEEDED
2 (9-inch) round pans or
  3 (6-inch) round pans

PREP TIME 10 minutes
BAKE TIME 20 to
  25 minutes

MAKES 2 (9-inch) rounds
  or 3 (6-inch) rounds
SERVES 4 to 6

This cake gets its intense flavor from a special addition of espresso powder, which really helps bring out the chocolate notes. You'll want to use a strong cocoa, like Dutch-processed or special dark, which can be found easily in most grocery stores. To make this vegan, I used a coconut yogurt, but any dairy alternative yogurt will do. I recommend using almond or soy for the plant-based milk in this recipe.

Nonstick baking spray
1 cup plant-based milk, at room
  temperature
1 teaspoon apple cider vinegar
1½ cups all-purpose flour
½ cup dark cocoa powder
1½ teaspoons baking soda
½ teaspoon baking powder

½ teaspoon salt
1¼ cups granulated sugar
¾ cup vegetable oil
1 teaspoon espresso powder
1 teaspoon hot water
½ cup vanilla or plain plant-based
  yogurt, at room temperature
Simple syrup (pages 12–13) (optional)

1. Preheat the oven to 350°F. Spray the pans with baking spray and set aside.

2. In a large bowl or measuring cup, combine the plant-based milk and vinegar. Give it a good stir and then set aside while you prepare the other ingredients.

3. In a large bowl, combine the flour, cocoa powder, baking soda, baking powder, and salt and whisk together. Set aside.

4. In another large bowl, whisk the sugar and oil together.

5. Dissolve the espresso powder in the hot water. Add the yogurt and the espresso mixture to the wet mixture. Combine well.

6. Add ½ cup of the milk mixture and whisk for about 10 seconds.

7. Sift half of the dry ingredients into the wet mixture and whisk well for about 15 seconds. Add in the rest of the milk mixture and the remainder of the dry ingredients. Use a rubber spatula to scrape down the sides of the bowl. Mix the batter for about 1 minute.

8. Divide the batter evenly into the prepared pans.

9. Bake for 20 to 22 minutes for the 9-inch rounds and 25 to 30 minutes for the 6-inch rounds, or until a toothpick inserted in the center comes out clean.

10. When cool enough to handle, remove the cakes from the pans, level, brush with the simple syrup (if using), tort, and chill before decorating.

VANILLA BUTTERCREAM

PREP TIME 10 minutes   MAKES 7 cups

There's nothing quite like a good old-fashioned vanilla cake. This buttercream recipe is my go-to for most of my decorating—not only for filling and stacking the cake, but also for frosting the outside. It's a lovely, pleasant, and fluffy buttercream that goes well with most fillings. It's also my choice for decorating cupcakes, because its white base is the perfect canvas for coloring.

3½ cups (7 sticks) salted butter, at room temperature

2 teaspoons vanilla extract

6½ cups confectioners' sugar, sifted

2 to 3 tablespoons heavy (whipping) cream

1. Cut each stick of butter into fourths and place in a large bowl or the bowl of a stand mixer.

2. Cream the butter on medium speed for 3 to 4 minutes, until it is light and fluffy and the color has changed to more of a whiteish shade.

3. Add in the vanilla and change the speed to the lowest setting. Slowly add the confectioners' sugar about 1 cup at a time.

4. Scrape down the sides of the bowl with a spatula to make sure that everything is well combined.

5. After you have added the last of the confectioners' sugar, add the heavy cream 1 tablespoon at a time. You may not need to use all of it, just enough to smooth out the buttercream a bit.

6. Store in an airtight container if you are not planning on using it right away. It can be left out at room temperature for up to 24 hours. If you plan on keeping it past that, refrigerate, or freeze for up to 1 month.

SWISS MERINGUE BUTTERCREAM

EQUIPMENT NEEDED
Candy thermometer
  or other food-safe
  thermometer

PREP TIME 5 minutes
COOK TIME 15 minutes
MAKES 5 cups

I really appreciate desserts that employ different flavor profiles and techniques and that are not too sweet. For this reason, I recommend trying an egg-based meringue buttercream. Made with granulated sugar instead of confectioners' sugar, this smooth, glossy, and fluffy buttercream is perfect for filling with and decorating. For visuals on this method, see the Vanilla de Leche (page 99) tutorial.

5 large egg whites, at room
  temperature but slightly cold
2 cups minus 1 tablespoon
  granulated sugar

1½ teaspoons vanilla extract
2½ cups (5 sticks) salted butter, at
  room temperature

1. Fill a 12- to 15-quart saucepan with an inch of water and bring to a low boil.

2. Put the egg whites and sugar in the bowl of a stand mixer and use a heat-resistant spatula to mix it for about 10 seconds. Scrape down the sides of bowl so that the granules stay together.

3. Place the mixing bowl on the saucepan right above the boiling water; the water should not be in direct contact with the bottom of the bowl.

4. Stir the sugar and egg white mixture slowly over the heat. The sugar granules should dissolve. Use the thermometer to check the temperature; it should not exceed 170°F. Keep stirring to avoid overcooking the eggs. If you do not have a thermometer, you can check if the sugar granules have dissolved by carefully rubbing a bit of the mixture between clean fingertips.

5. After the sugar has dissolved, set the bowl on the stand mixer, and using the whisk attachment, mix on medium speed for 1 minute, then turn the speed up a level higher. If you are using a handheld, whisk directly in the bowl.

CONTINUED >

6. As the whites thicken, watch for a stiff, sticky texture. You can do this by stopping the mixer and seeing if the whites wisp off the whisk and hold their shape. At this point, add the vanilla.

7. Whisk until the bowl has cooled to room temperature, or until the egg whites come to a medium to stiff glossy peak. Set the speed to medium.

8. Slowly add the butter, 1 to 2 tablespoons at a time; wait at least 10 seconds before adding the next bit. The mixture will look a bit loose but will stiffen as soon as all the butter has been added.

9. As soon as the last of the butter is added, set the speed to high and mix for 10 to 15 seconds. The finished product should be glossy, fluffy, and stable.

10. Store in an airtight container if you are not planning on using it right away. It can be left out at room temperature for up to 24 hours. If you plan on keeping it past that, refrigerate, or freeze for up to 1 month.

VEGAN CHOCOLATE BUTTERCREAM

PREP TIME 10 minutes   **MAKES** 4 cups

Believe it or not, this is one of my favorite chocolate buttercream recipes. Its rich, decadent chocolate flavor also goes well with non-vegan cakes. Its texture is creamy and smooth, perfect for frosting. Most plant-based butters should be suitable for this recipe. I have found that the one offered by Country Crock is the best for the smoothest, creamiest vegan chocolate buttercream you'll ever have.

2 cups plant-based butter, cold

¾ cup dark chocolate chips

3½ cups confectioners' sugar, divided

¼ cup dark cocoa powder

½ teaspoon salt

1. Place the butter in a microwave-safe bowl and heat in the microwave for 10 seconds, then give it a slight squeeze to see if it is softened. You are looking for a slightly cold and still firm but soft feel.

2. Transfer the butter to a mixing bowl and cream on low speed for 2 to 3 minutes. You do not want to overmix this kind of butter as it tends to soften more quickly.

3. After you cream the butter, melt the chocolate chips in a microwave-safe bowl in the microwave for 30 seconds. Check to see if they have begun to melt and give it a slow stir. Heat them up for another 15 seconds, check and stir again, and heat up in intervals of 10 seconds if needed. When the chocolate has a shine to it, you should stir/temper it slowly. Set the melted chocolate aside.

4. Sift in 1 cup of the confectioners' sugar and all of the cocoa powder to the creamed butter. Beat with a mixer on low speed for 30 seconds. Add the salt.

5. Add in the melted chocolate, then the remaining 2 ½ cups of confectioners' sugar in small amounts. Beat on medium speed until fluffy for 1 to 2 minutes.

6. If not using right away, store in an airtight container in the refrigerator for up to 1 month.

CREAM CHEESE FROSTING

PREP TIME 10 minutes   MAKES 5 cups

A classic cream cheese frosting is somehow always the best with all kinds of bakes. Whether you're pairing it with red velvet, carrot cake, or chocolate, it remains a fluffy and delicious frosting with vanilla notes. It's a little tangy and not overly sweet, which makes it a great complement for spiced cakes and anything with fruit. Although this can be made in a stand mixer, the handheld with the whisk attachment is recommended because it makes it easier to beat the cream cheese.

1½ cups (3 sticks) salted butter, at room temperature

4 ounces cream cheese, at room temperature

1 teaspoon vanilla extract

4 cups confectioners' sugar, sifted

1. In a large bowl, using a handheld mixer on medium speed, cream the butter and cream cheese together for about 2 minutes, until fluffy.

2. Add the vanilla and mix well.

3. Sift in 1 cup of the confectioners' sugar and beat on medium speed until combined. Add in the rest of the confectioners' sugar by the cupful. The frosting should be fluffy and creamy.

4. If not using right away, store in an airtight container in the refrigerator for up to 2 weeks.

WHIPPED CREAM FROSTING

PREP TIME 10 minutes   MAKES 4 cups

This is a stabilized whipped cream recipe, which means that it should hold its shape and should be able to withstand sitting out for a few hours. Sometimes I'll get a request for a cake covered in whipped cream, and I turn to this recipe to accomplish that. You can flavor it with any extract, but I'm a big fan of a vanilla-based one, because it goes well with most bakes. It is important to follow the instructions in the order that they are so that you do not end up with chunky, thick whipped cream.

2 teaspoons gelatin powder

2 teaspoons cold water

2 cups heavy (whipping) cream

1 teaspoon vanilla extract

½ cup confectioners' sugar

1. In a small bowl, mix the gelatin and water together and let the gelatin bloom for 3 minutes. It should be somewhat thick.

2. While the gelatin is blooming, in a large mixing bowl, combine the heavy cream and vanilla.

3. After the gelatin has bloomed, begin whipping the cream with a stand mixer or handheld mixer using the whisk attachment. Whisk on medium speed for 30 seconds, then add the confectioners' sugar and whisk for another 30 seconds.

4. Meanwhile, warm up the gelatin in the microwave for 10 seconds first, give it a stir, then another 10 seconds. Give it another stir; it should have the consistency of a syrup.

5. When the whipping cream has reached the soft peak stage, where it is thick but does not hold shape, slowly add the warm gelatin.

6. Adjust the speed to high and let the cream reach the medium peak stage, then switch back to medium speed and whisk for another 20 to 30 seconds. Stop and check if the cream sticks to the whisk and holds its shape. Try not to over-whisk.

7. If not using right away, store in an airtight container in the refrigerator for up to 1 week.

HOMEMADE MARSHMALLOW FONDANT

EQUIPMENT NEEDED
Silicon baking mat

PREP TIME 10 minutes

MAKES Enough fondant to cover a 6-inch round, 3-tiered cake

Although there are many brands that carry decent-tasting fondant, nothing beats homemade marshmallow fondant. You can customize its taste by using any clear flavoring (anything without dyes or color) of choice. You may cover cakes and cupcakes, create toppers, and use it in various other ways to add details to your cakes. If you are not using it right away, double wrap the fondant, place it in a zip-top bag, and store it in a cool, dry place for up to 5 days.

4 cups mini marshmallows
3 cups confectioners' sugar, divided

1 teaspoon vegetable shortening

1. Put the marshmallows in a microwave-safe bowl and heat on high for 20 seconds. Check to see if they have started to puff up and melt. If the top of the marshmallows has expanded and looks very fluffy, go ahead and stir them to combine.

2. Spread 1 cup of confectioners' sugar on the baking mat.

3. Pour the melted marshmallows over the sugar and use a spatula to scrape all of the marshmallow out of the bowl.

4. Use the spatula to fold the marshmallows and confectioners' sugar together on the mat. Use a motion like you're spreading butter on a slice of bread, then flip your hand and do the motion the other way.

5. Add another cup of confectioners' sugar and repeat the folding motion this way.

6. You'll start to notice the marshmallows sticking to the mat. At this point, put on gloves and grease your hands with a bit of the shortening. Add the last cup of powdered sugar and work it into the sticky fondant.

7. Proceed to mix the marshmallows and confectioners' sugar with a stretching and pulling motion with your hands until all of the confectioners' sugar is combined. The fondant should be firm but easily pliable.

8. If not using right away, store in an airtight container at room temperature.

CHOCOLATE GANACHE

PREP TIME 5 minutes, plus 2 hours to rest

COOK TIME 2–3 minutes

MAKES 2 cups; enough to fill a cake or frost 12 cupcakes

For the ultimate chocolate lover out there, a smooth and thick chocolate ganache can do no wrong. Ganache can be made in different consistencies to serve different purposes. For instance, you'll want a thinner one to do a drip on a cake and a thicker one to frost a cake. This recipe will result in a decadent, thick ganache that is perfect for filling and frosting cakes or cupcakes. In chapter 4 (Chocolate Decadence, page 75), you'll be making a thinner ganache to spread over the top of a chocolate cake, so you'll soon have both in your repertoire.

1⅔ cups dark chocolate chips
1½ cups heavy (whipping) cream

1 tablespoon salted butter, at room temperature

1. Place the chocolate chips in a glass measuring cup.

2. In a large saucepan, heat the heavy cream over low heat, stirring occasionally to avoid a skin forming on top. When small bubbles start to form at the edges, heat for another 20 seconds and then remove from the heat.

3. Pour the cream over the chocolate chips and make sure they are entirely covered. Let it sit for 1 minute.

4. Use a small whisk to combine the chocolate and cream. Now stir in the butter. It will look milky until everything is combined. The finished product should be a thick, shiny, and dark ganache.

5. Take a piece of plastic wrap and set it right on top of the ganache so that it is touching it. This helps to prevent a skin from forming. Set aside for at least 2 hours before using, or set in the refrigerator.

6. To get a lighter texture that helps with frosting a cake, beat the chilled ganache with a whisk attachment on medium speed for 1 to 2 minutes.

7. If not using right away, store in an airtight container in the refrigerator for up to 2 weeks.

VEGAN CHOCOLATE GANACHE

PREP TIME 5 minutes,
plus 2 hours to rest   **COOK TIME** 2-3 minutes   **MAKES** 2 cups

This ganache is great for filling a vegan cake and can also be used to fill and frost cupcakes. It's super simple to make with only two ingredients and is perfect when looking for a quick chocolate fix. It's smooth and velvety like a regular chocolate ganache and can be used as a substitute when you need a nondairy chocolate dessert.

1½ cups dark vegan chocolate   1 cup canned coconut cream

1. Place the dark vegan chocolate in a glass measuring cup.

2. Open the can of coconut cream and scrape ONLY the solid portion out into a 12- to 15-quart saucepan. Discard or reserve the liquid for something else.

3. Heat the coconut cream on low heat. It should start to become liquid. Wait for boiling around the edges and then give it a good stir. Wait about 20 seconds before removing from the heat and pouring over the dark chocolate.

4. Make sure all the chocolate has been covered by the cream and let sit for 1 minute.

5. After 1 minute, whisk until well combined. You should have a thick, glossy, and dark ganache that is consistent throughout.

6. Take a piece of plastic wrap and place it directly on top of the ganache so that it is touching it. Set aside for at least 2 hours before using. You may speed up the process of cooling by putting it in the refrigerator.

7. If not using right away, store in an airtight container in the refrigerator for up to 2 weeks.

CAKE DECORATING 101

My first cake was not spectacular . . . it was quite the opposite. Looking back, I realize I attempted too many things at once: a border, chocolate decorations, and a drip. But as I looked at the scraggly sides and melty drip, I knew that I wanted to learn how to be better. I invested in a turntable and picked up my piping bags. It took plenty of practice, but eventually I transformed my awkward first cake into a smooth, beautifully decorated creation.

Based on my experience, I have put together the basics for you to learn so that with practice and patience, your cakes will be ready for any occasion.

···FROSTING A CAKE···

While learning how to assemble and decorate layered cakes, you may come across different techniques for frosting a cake and getting it ready for final decoration. I will share with you the methods I have found to be best for achieving smooth cake "bellies" and getting those sharp edges on top of the cake. After preparing the basic building blocks—those yummy cake layers—there are a few tricks to frosting a cake nicely before putting on those final touches. You will start leveling the layers after baking and finish off with a pristine-looking buttercream cake ready for embellishment.

Leveling Cake Layers

The first important step is cutting off any domes that may appear on the cake layers after baking while the cakes are still warm but cool enough to handle. Domes are natural puffiness or extra height on cakes that occur due to certain things like heat and structure of the batter in recipes. Cutting off the dome leaves you with a layer that has a flat surface. This way, you can avoid a wobbly cake because you're stacking even layers of rounds. There are some fancy levelers on the market; however, you can easily access the two tools shown in the pictures.

1. To use a wire leveler, set the wire at the notches of your desired cake thickness and move the wire in a sawing motion through the cake. The legs of the leveler should remain in contact with the surface you are cutting the cake on. After you have leveled the top, give it a nice brushing with simple syrup. You can save the trimmings for cake pops or cakesicles, but just make sure you give them a light brushing of simple syrup as well. Wrap with plastic wrap and store in the freezer or refrigerator for at least 30 minutes or up to 2 days.

2. To level using a cake or bread knife (both have a similar function), hold the cake gently on the top and decide on the height of the layer. Use a gentle horizontal sawing motion and keep the knife as straight as you can while cutting across the cake. If your cut is slightly uneven, split the difference by cutting across at the highest point and continue the straight cut.

Torting Cake Layers

While leveling and torting may seem like the same thing, they are two different steps. Torting is an optional technique to be done after you have leveled off the cake dome. If the cake layer is thicker than 2 inches, you may wish to divide the leveled layer into two. This helps ensure even distribution of the cake and filling components during stacking. However, you can use the same tools of choice that you used for leveling: the wire leveler or cake/bread knife. Simply follow the guidelines for leveling, but make sure you cut the cake into equal halves.

1. First remove the top portion just as you would when leveling.

2. If you are using a wire leveler, set the wire at the notch that is the halfway point of the cake height.

3. Gently hold the cake in place as you smoothly saw the cake in half with the wire leveler.

You can use a similar method with a cake or bread knife, just make sure to find the halfway point of the cake layer using a ruler.

Filling and Stacking Cake Layers

After preparing cake layers, you will have to decide if you want to stack them frozen or at room temperature. I prefer to freeze my layers right after leveling and torting. When the cake is frozen, the buttercream firms up quickly as you build upon the layers. It makes for a very stable cake that is easy to work with. However, working with room-temperature layers is also possible if you do not have time to freeze them. Just follow this technique and you will have a cake ready for crumb coating.

1. Apply a very thin layer of buttercream on a cake board to help set the first layer of cake. The diameter should not be larger than the cake itself.

Cake boards come in many forms, including cardboard, foam, acrylic, and plastic. The one pictured here is called a "drum" which is a foam disc wrapped in food-safe foil.

2. Set the first layer on the board over the buttercream. Spread and push it down enough so that the layer is level.

3. Using a palette knife, spread a generous amount of buttercream on the layer and spin the turntable to push the buttercream around evenly.

4. Repeat for each layer except for the top one. You will also want to make sure the layers are evened up and there are no gaps in the buttercream layers. You can fill in gaps with a palette knife and smooth over the entire cake with a cake comb as a precursor to crumb coating.

Crumb Coating a Cake

I highly recommend completing this before putting on the final coat of buttercream. We call this step "crumb coating" because a thin layer of buttercream is applied to the cake to "lock" any loose crumbs in. I prefer to do this after the stacked cake has had time to cool in the refrigerator and the layers have hardened. If you are pressed for time, you may apply a crumb coat at room temperature. However, like stacking, crumb coating a cold cake will be much easier. Follow these guidelines to prepare the cake for its final coat of buttercream.

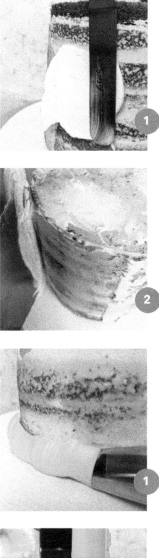

1. Use a palette knife or scraper to apply a thin layer of buttercream on the stacked cake.

2. Scrape the buttercream over the cake. Fill in any areas of cake that are exposed so that the crumbs are locked in by the frosting.

Smooth Frosting a Cake

One of the goals for many decorators is to achieve a smooth cake with no air bubbles or rough texture. If you have followed all of the steps from leveling to crumb coating, you have set yourself up for success. It takes a bit of practice, but after you get the hang of it, there is no better feeling than scraping the buttercream to a smooth finish.

1. Fit a piping bag with a frosting tip (I used a ruffle tip) and spin the turntable as you drag a layer of frosting around the cake. Work your way from the bottom until the cake is covered, including the top of the cake.

2. Rotate the turntable and use a large palette knife to smooth down the frosting that you piped. This is your preliminary step before using a comb.

3. Using an offset spatula, rotate the turntable and spread the buttercream evenly over the top of the cake. Depending on what hand is dominant, you should be turning the table toward you and pushing the spatula in the opposite direction.

4. Rotate the turntable away from you while using your dominant hand to scrape a cake comb toward you. The frosting will smoothen out with each scrape. Be careful not to scrape so much that the crumb coat is revealed.

5. Use a small offset spatula to patch up holes in the buttercream.

6. After the patchwork, scrape the cake surface again a few more times. Fill in any holes that appear during these last few scrapes. Repeat this smoothing process until you are satisfied with the final coat.

A few trips to the refrigerator are essential if you want to achieve a very smooth coat of buttercream. This helps with the patchwork and smoothing-over process. I usually do a couple rounds of this before becoming satisfied with my final coat.

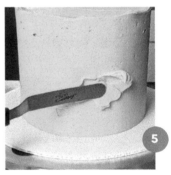

A metal scraper is good to have, because you can heat it up by running the edge under hot water and using it for the last few scrapes for a very smooth finish. Make sure you only scrape a few times with the comb hot, as too many uses can form bubbles in the buttercream.

• • • PASTRY BAG BASICS • • •

My favorite part about decorating is piping. You can use a wide variety of piping tips to create everything from the smallest detail to the fluffiest border. Each tip allows for a lot of flexibility in its results, depending on how you use it. And yes, there is a technique for using each tip. It takes a little bit of practice, but once you are comfortable with piping, decorating gorgeous cakes and cupcakes will be effortless.

You will also want to pair the tip with the right size of pastry bag. For instance, if you want to pipe small detail, a 6-inch bag would do just fine. If you are filling cake layers or piping a big border, then a 12- or 24-inch bag would suffice. You can also find sizes in between, as they can usually be found in increments of 2 inches.

Another item to consider is whether to use disposable or reusable pastry bags. Environmental factors are in favor of reusable bags. For convenience, disposable bags can be tossed after a single use, and you will have less to clean up. Personally, a decent quantity of disposable bags that I wash with hot water and reuse has worked for me. If you are going the reusable route, the most common ones you'll find will be made from canvas or silicone.

When it comes to choosing piping tips, you may want to start with a few basics and then branch out to smaller or larger versions. A lot of companies offer a starter kit with 12 to 16 different basic tips. The most common ones are star tips, leaf tips, round tips, drop flower tips, ruffle tips, and petal tips.

Prepping and Filling a Pastry Bag

The most effective method of filling a pastry bag is to use a tall cup. I've even used a flower vase for filling a 24-inch bag. Smaller bags are less tricky to fill and can easily be done by holding the bag in your hand. Before filling the bag, do two things: stir the air bubbles out of the frosting and fit the piping tip in the bag. The second step may seem a bit intuitive, but there are times that I've completely forgotten to do so before filling the bag! After those steps, the rest is easy.

1. Gather the bags and tips you intend to use, along with a tall glass and pair of scissors. Insert the piping tip in the narrow end of an uncut bag. Let it fit snugly.

2. Push the tip back a bit and cut the bag near the opening of the piping tip, just enough so that the features of the tip are exposed. You may want to start cutting the smallest opening and then gradually cut to the size you want.

3. Push the tip through the opening. The widest part of the piping tip should not slide past the opening that you cut.

4. Place the piping bag in the glass tip-side down and roll the larger opening down over the sides of the glass.

5. Scoop the frosting into the bag with a spatula or spoon. Do not overfill, as you will have trouble twisting the opening close when ready for piping.

6. Lift the bag out of the glass and gently nudge the frosting down by holding the top corners and shaking up and down lightly.

You may also use your hand to hold the piping bag like a cone and scoop the frosting into the bag. Having the edges folded over is also helpful.

Piping with Flourish

With the right technique, you can embellish cakes and cupcakes as if you were writing in script. We will start with a basic and popular tip–the 1M or large open star. If this is unavailable to you, a closed star or 2D has a similar effect. With these you can make beautiful rosettes and even level up to piping Lambeth-style borders. All it takes is getting used to the pressure and release of piping bags.

1. Hold a bag with one hand to pipe. Twist the large opening a few times so that the buttercream stays in the bag. Hold the twisted area between the index finger and thumb of your dominant hand. The bag should be resting on the rest of your hand as seen here.

2. Practice first! Hold the tip straight over a flat surface. Choose your starting point and start to squeeze the bag at medium strength.

3. From your starting point, the center of the rosette, circle the tip around in a counterclockwise fashion as you grow the rosette. This is a gentle motion and uses the right balance of pace and pressure. Finish by letting go of your hand squeeze. The rosette ending should have a narrow tail.

4. Now pipe rosettes onto the cake in the form of a border, a cascade design, or directly onto cupcakes.

Piping Sweet and Simple Stars

Although they may seem basic, stars can add a fun look to a cake. Dragging an open star tip can also make for a dramatic effect such as a pretty border or exaggerated texture. A quick squeeze combined with a gentle pull away/release will make the prettiest star. To achieve a perfect star, hover the tip over the exact spot where you want it to appear. It is best to hold the bag straight up and down so that the star has a clear center point. A small drag and quick release is called shell piping.

1. Point the tip straight down and hover just above the surface that you want to pipe on. Use a small, gentle squeeze to pipe the star shape.

2. To close the star, lift up gently but quickly at the peak, or center, of the star.

3. To pipe a shell border, rotate the turntable away from you while squeezing the star shape and elongating it horizontally. Pipe toward the left, pull the frosting up, and bring it down by the board. The motion should feel like you are writing a question mark on its side.

4. Shell piping starts off wide and ends narrow as you drag the tip down to start the next segment.

···WORKING WITH FONDANT···

Both edible and pliable, fondant is a great medium to use for a few reasons. With the right tools, you can cover a cake with it, create toppers, add texture, and manipulate it to make tiny details. Fondant can also be colored and painted on, making it a favorite choice for decorators who have those skills in their repertoire. And for those who enjoy sculptural cakes, fondant is the perfect edible material to work with. It can also withstand outdoor environments slightly better than buttercream.

While there are many kinds of fondant, nothing beats Homemade Marshmallow Fondant (page 34). After I realized I could make my own fondant at home, I started to enjoy working with it more often. I use it for shape molds and to cut out small details. There are specific fondant cutters out there, but if you have a cookie cutter, that would work fine as well.

Cutting Out Decorative Shapes

You may use cutters, molds, and even impression mats to create details and effects. Fondant is popular among those who make realistic flowers. It does not stop at cakes, however, and you may use fondant pieces as cupcake and cakesicle toppers as well. You will want to use a small amount for the molds, as you will probably have to fit the fondant bits in. For rolling out fondant to be cut, the

best tool is a rolling pin that has thickness rings affixed to it. This way, the thickness of the fondant is consistent as you cut out shapes.

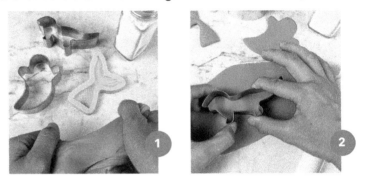

1. Work fondant by pulling it like taffy and then place it on a flat surface lightly dusted with cornstarch. Use a roller to flatten it to the desired thickness.

2. Place the cutter over the fondant and press down firmly so that it cuts all the way through. Remove the edges from around the cutter to reveal the shape.

Covering a Cake with Fondant

To cover a cake, you will need a large rolling pin, a blade, cornstarch, 20 to 25 ounces of fondant, and a fully iced, cold cake. You will also want to invest in some fondant smoothers, which help get rid of unwanted creases and wrinkles in the fondant. The reason why you want an iced and very cold cake (preferably with time to set overnight) is because then you will have a drier surface to apply the fondant to. Take your time and know that there is a learning curve for applying fondant. This technique is universal and a very basic way to start.

1. Start by working the fondant. Knead, pull, and twist it so that it is very pliable. If it sticks to your hands, apply a little cornstarch to the sticky area.

2. Roll the fondant with a large rolling pin. Most fondant rollers have bands so that you roll it out at a consistent thickness. Dust with cornstarch when necessary, such as when the fondant sticks to the surface of the rolling pin.

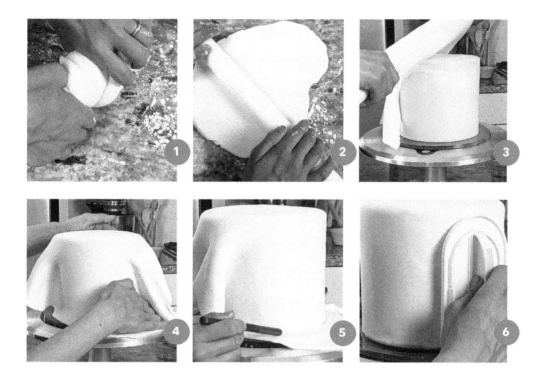

It is better to have extra fondant than to have less when covering a cake. If you are unsure about measurements, take the dimensions of the cake to determine how big of a piece of fondant you want to roll out.

3. Roll the pin and fondant together so that the fondant is wrapped around the pin. Use this method to transport the fondant in one piece over to the cake. As you unroll the fondant from the pin, drape the large piece over the cake.

4. Smooth out the excess and pleats in a horizontal fashion. Avoid pulling it down to reach the board as this will stretch out the fondant and it will rip. Instead, use a gentle pulling and smoothing motion as you make your way around the cake.

5. Use a sharp blade to trim the excess fondant at the base of the cake on the board.

6. Use smoothers to gently flatten the surfaces and press out wrinkles.

If you are new to cake decorating, sheet cakes are a great place to start. Over the next few pages, you will find a delicious variety of tray bakes (the other common name for sheet cakes) that are easily put together and all have a unique look of their own. Mastering these cakes will help prepare you for the next adventure: baking and decorating layer cakes!

SHEET CAKES

BANOFFEE SNACK CAKE

EQUIPMENT NEEDED
9-by-13-inch pan
Palette knife
1 small piping bag
3 or 5 (round) piping tip

PREP TIME 10 minutes
BAKE TIME 30 to 35 minutes
DECORATING TIME 10 minutes
MAKES 1 (9-by-13-inch) sheet cake
SERVES 10 to 15

The classic English dessert gets a cake makeover in this recipe. A pool of warm dulce de leche is poured over a moist and dense banana cake to create the base. A dulce de leche buttercream and fresh banana slices then finish off this delicious tray bake. You can substitute caramel sauce if you cannot find dulce de leche at the store.

Nonstick baking spray
3 ripe bananas, divided
1 cup packed brown sugar
½ cup granulated sugar
¾ cup vegetable oil
½ cup plain full-fat yogurt
½ cup whole milk

1½ cups all-purpose flour
1 teaspoon baking soda
½ teaspoon salt
1¼ cups dulce de leche, divided
1 cup (2 sticks) salted butter
2 cups confectioners' sugar
½ teaspoon salt

1. Preheat the oven to 350°F. Spray the pan with baking spray and set aside.

2. Slice 2 bananas and place them in a large mixing bowl. Mash the bananas with a fork until they are soft, though they will still look lumpy.

3. Pour in the brown sugar and granulated sugar and combine.

4. Add the oil and mix well. Next, add in the yogurt and combine well. Add the milk and mix again.

5. In a separate bowl, mix the flour, baking soda, and salt together. Add the flour mixture to the wet mixture and whisk until incorporated.

6. Pour the batter into the prepared pan. Bake for 30 to 35 minutes, or until a toothpick inserted into the center comes out clean.

7. In a heat-safe measuring cup, heat ½ cup of the dulce de leche in the microwave for 10-second intervals, until it is easy to stir with a spoon.

CONTINUED >

8. Pour the warm dulce de leche onto the cake. Spread it evenly with a palette knife.

9. Chill the cake for 20 minutes while you prepare the buttercream.

10. To make the buttercream: Using a mixer, cream the butter on low speed for 2 minutes until light and fluffy.

11. Add ½ cup of dulce de leche and beat on medium speed for 1 minute.

12. Sift in the confectioners' sugar and salt. Beat on medium speed for 2 minutes until smooth.

13. Spread the buttercream over the chilled cake evenly with a palette knife.

14. Slice up the last banana and place the slices randomly on the buttercream.

15. In a small heat-safe bowl, heat the remaining ¼ cup of dulce de leche and put it in a small piping bag fitted with the small round tip. Drizzle, draw, and be creative.

TRES LECHES CAKE

EQUIPMENT NEEDED
9-by-13-inch pan
Palette knife
2 (4-by-12-inch or bigger) piping bags
1M (large star) and 8B (open star)
  piping tips

PREP TIME 20 minutes
BAKE TIME 30 to 35 minutes
DECORATING TIME 10 minutes
MAKES 1 (9-by-13-inch) sheet cake
SERVES 20

This cake, whose name translates to "three milks," is best served with extra liquid. The cake will soak up the liquid right away, so try to have extra on hand for presentation. Double the recipe below for the milk mixture if you plan on serving a day or so after it is made. Your guests who know and love this traditional cake will love the fruit toppings, whipped cream, and sweet milks that soak into the cake.

FOR THE CAKE
Nonstick baking spray
2½ cups all-purpose flour
½ teaspoon baking powder
1 teaspoon baking soda
½ teaspoon salt
1 cup (2 sticks) salted butter, at room
  temperature
¼ cup canola or vegetable oil

1¾ cups granulated sugar
2 large eggs
1 large egg yolk
1 teaspoon vanilla extract
½ cup sour cream
1 cup whole milk
¼ cup evaporated milk

FOR THE MILK MIXTURE
1 cup condensed milk
1 cup evaporated milk
1 cup whole milk

½ teaspoon vanilla extract
½ teaspoon ground cinnamon
  (optional)

FOR THE WHIPPED TOPPING
3 cups heavy (whipping) cream
½ cup confectioners' sugar

1 teaspoon vanilla extract

FOR THE TOPPINGS
3 peaches (skin on, for color)
1½ cups strawberries
½ cup granulated sugar

¼ teaspoon ground cinnamon
Sprinkles

CONTINUED >

1. Preheat the oven to 350°F. Spray the pan with baking spray and set aside.

2. To make the cake: In a bowl, combine the dry ingredients: flour, baking powder, baking soda, and salt and whisk together. Set aside.

3. Using a mixer, mix the butter, oil, and sugar together for 1 minute on low speed, then add the eggs, egg yolk, vanilla, sour cream, whole milk, and evaporated milk.

4. Sift the dry ingredients into the wet mixture and combine well for about 2 minutes on low speed.

5. Pour the batter into the prepared pan and bake for 30 to 35 minutes, or until a toothpick inserted into the center comes out clean.

6. Right out of the oven, use a fork to poke holes about half an inch apart on the cake. Set aside to cool.

7. To make the milk mixture: In a bowl, combine the condensed milk, evaporated milk, whole milk, and vanilla. If you choose to use cinnamon, add it now and mix well. Pour the mixture over the cake and let it soak in.

8. To make the whipped topping: Using a mixer, combine the heavy cream, confectioners' sugar, and vanilla on high speed until stiff peaks are achieved.

9. When the cake has cooled, use an ice cream scoop to distribute half the whipped cream evenly over the cake and spread with a palette knife.

10. Put the rest of the whipped cream into two piping bags fitted with piping tips.

11. Pipe rosettes with the 1M tip. Pipe stars with the other 8B tip.

12. To make the topping: Cut the peaches into eighths and halve the strawberries. In a 12- to 15-quart saucepan, combine the peaches, sugar, and cinnamon and simmer on low heat for 10 minutes. Let cool completely.

13. Arrange the fruit on top of the cake.

14. Finish with some colorful sprinkles.

COOKIE BUTTER CAKE

EQUIPMENT NEEDED
9-by-13-inch pan
Palette knife
2 (4-by-12-inch or bigger) piping bags
1M (large star) and 4B (open star)
  piping tips

PREP TIME 20 minutes
BAKE TIME 30 to 35 minutes
DECORATING TIME 10 minutes
MAKES 1 (9-by-13-inch) sheet cake
SERVES 20

If you've ever had the opportunity to enjoy Biscoff cookies, then you know the magic of a speculoos cookie. The best part is that you can find all the Biscoff flavor in a jar in the form of cookie butter. A mixture of warm spices and caramel notes makes this widely popular cookie a favorite ingredient for many bakers. This cake takes all those wonderful warm flavors and transforms the iconic cookie into cake form for the ultimate cookie butter fan. Look for Biscoff spread or cookie butter in the peanut butter section of a well-stocked grocery store.

FOR THE CAKE
Nonstick baking spray
2¼ cups all-purpose flour
1½ teaspoons baking soda
¼ teaspoon salt
1¾ cups granulated sugar

1 cup (2 sticks) salted butter, melted
2 large eggs
½ cup cookie butter
1¼ cups whole milk
Simple syrup (pages 12–13)

FOR THE BUTTERCREAM
1½ cups (3 sticks) salted butter, at
  room temperature
⅓ cup cookie butter, at room
  temperature

3¼ cups confectioners' sugar, sifted
1 to 2 teaspoons heavy
  (whipping) cream

FOR THE BISCOFF GLAZE
¾ cup white chocolate chips, divided

½ cup cookie butter, melted

FOR DECORATING
10 to 12 strawberries
1 cup dark chocolate, melted

5 or 6 Biscoff cookies

CONTINUED >

1. Preheat the oven to 350°F. Spray the pan with baking spray and set aside.

2. To make the cake: In a bowl, combine the flour, baking soda, and salt, and set aside.

3. In another bowl, combine the sugar and melted butter. Mix with a whisk until well combined.

4. Add the eggs to the bowl and mix until well incorporated.

5. Heat the cookie butter in increments of 15 seconds in the microwave until warm and melted. Mix it into the wet mixture.

6. Add the milk to the wet mixture and mix well.

7. Add in the flour mixture, slowly at first (try not to dump it all in). Mix until the batter is smooth and there are few to no lumps.

8. Pour the batter into the prepared pan. Bake for 30 to 35 minutes, or until a toothpick inserted into the center comes out clean.

9. Brush the simple syrup over the top of the cake when it is fresh out of the oven.

10. To make the buttercream: Using a mixer, cream the butter on low speed until whitish and fluffy. If using a stand mixer, use the paddle attachment. If using a handheld mixer, use the beaters.

11. On medium speed, add the cookie butter and slowly add the confectioners' sugar.

12. Add the heavy cream and beat until the frosting is fluffy and smooth.

13. Using a large palette knife, spread 1½ cups of frosting onto the cake. You may also use a tall cake scraper to smooth it out evenly.

14. Put half of the remaining buttercream into a bag fitted with a 1M tip and pipe a border around the cake.

15. Put the rest of the buttercream into a bag fitted with a 4B tip and pipe another border. Chill the cake for 20 minutes.

16. To make the glaze: Melt ½ cup of white chocolate and stir it into the cookie butter. Pour it over the chilled cake.

17. Melt the remaining ¼ cup of white chocolate, then fill a squeeze bottle with it. Draw lines with it horizontally on the cake.

18. Starting at one end of the horizontal lines, use a toothpick to drag the white chocolate in one direction, then switch directions and drag the other way.

19. Decorate the top with chocolate-dipped fruit and Biscoff cookies, if you like.

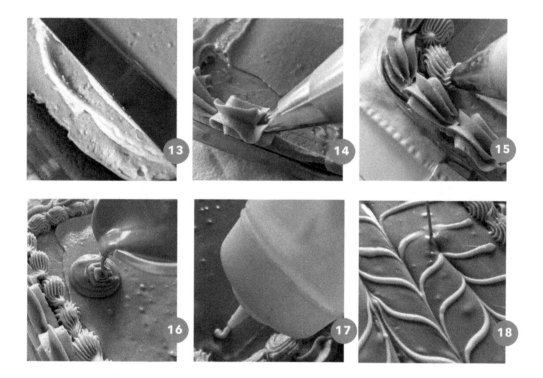

TIRAMISU SWISS ROLL

EQUIPMENT NEEDED
9-by-13-inch pan
Palette knife

PREP TIME 15 minutes
BAKE TIME 15 minutes
DECORATING TIME 5 minutes
MAKES 1 Swiss roll
SERVES 8 to 10

A cake that is sure to impress your guests is a Swiss roll full of rich coffee flavor and a delicate mascarpone filling. The traditional tiramisu flavors are quite noticeable in this cake, and the filling-to-sponge ratio shows off a beautiful, perfect swirl. I love serving this with a cup of coffee or milk and a little touch of espresso syrup to drizzle over the top.

FOR THE CAKE
Nonstick baking spray
1¼ cups cake flour
1 teaspoon baking powder
¼ teaspoon salt
1½ tablespoons espresso powder
1½ tablespoons hot water
3 tablespoons whole milk

½ teaspoon vanilla extract
¼ cup vegetable oil
½ cup granulated sugar
2 large egg whites
¼ teaspoon cream of tartar
2 tablespoons confectioners' sugar

FOR THE FILLING
½ cup mascarpone, cold
1 teaspoon vanilla extract

1½ cups heavy (whipping) cream, cold
⅔ cup confectioners' sugar

FOR SERVING
1 tablespoon espresso powder
2 tablespoons hot water

¼ cup condensed milk

CONTINUED >

1. Preheat the oven to 325°F. Spray the pan with baking spray and set aside.

2. To make the cake: In a bowl, combine the flour, baking powder, and salt, whisk, and set aside.

3. In a small measuring cup, dissolve the espresso powder in the hot water. Add the milk and vanilla.

4. In a separate bowl, mix the oil and granulated sugar together until well combined, then add the liquid coffee mixture. Sift in the dry ingredients and mix well.

5. Using a mixer with a whisk attachment, beat the egg whites and cream of tartar on medium then high speed. Beat until the whites are fluffy and have stiff peaks.

6. Fold the egg whites into the batter, using a gentle motion so all the air does not get knocked out.

7. Pour the mixture into the prepared pan. Bake for 15 minutes, or until a toothpick inserted into the center comes out clean.

8. While the cake is still warm, sprinkle the confectioners' sugar over the cake.

9. While the cake is warm, roll up the cake from one end to the other. Do this gently. Let cool for 15 to 20 minutes.

10. To make the filling: While you are waiting for the cake to cool, fit the mixer with the whisk attachment. Beat the mascarpone and vanilla on medium speed until smooth and creamy. Add in half of the cream. Sift in the confectioners' sugar, then beat on high speed. When the mixture has thickened, add the remaining half of the whipping cream. Beat until the filling is fluffy and well combined.

11. Unroll the cake and use a palette knife to spread the filling over the entirety of the cake.

12. Re-roll the cake so that the filling and cake are wrapped up together. You should be able to see a nice swirl.

13. To serve: Mix the espresso powder with the water, and then mix in the condensed milk. You can spoon it onto a plate for the cake to lay on when serving. It adds a nice strong coffee taste just like real tiramisu!

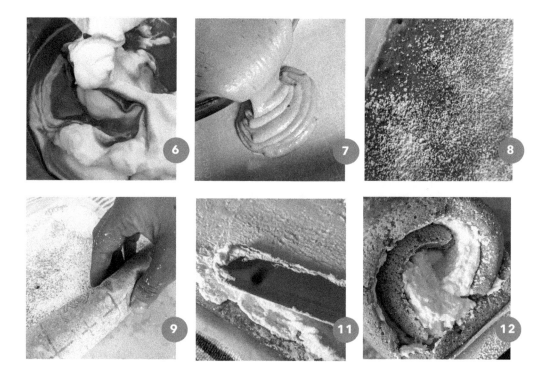

MINI LEMON AND OLIVE OIL CAKES WITH BLACKBERRIES AND ALMOND BUTTERCREAM

EQUIPMENT NEEDED
2 (9-by-13-inch) pans
2 (12-inch) piping bags
1 large star piping tip (of the B variety)
  and 1A (round) piping tip
Tweezer

PREP TIME 15 minutes
BAKE TIME 20 to 25 minutes
DECORATING TIME 15 minutes
MAKES 6 mini cakes

Since this chapter focuses on sheet cakes, I wanted to share a variety of styles in which they can be served. These mini cakes are a fun way to spruce up a standard sheet cake and serve them with tea or refreshments. Personal-size portions of bright and summery lemon olive oil cake are paired with a smooth almond buttercream and flavorful blackberry sauce. They'll not only be the most delicious dessert at a gathering but will look charming on the table as well.

FOR THE CAKE
Nonstick baking spray
2 cups all-purpose flour
2 cups cake flour
1 teaspoon baking soda
½ teaspoon baking powder
½ teaspoon salt
1 cup (2 sticks) salted butter, at room
  temperature
1¾ cups granulated sugar

½ cup olive oil
¼ cup vegetable oil
2 large eggs, at room temperature
½ cup plain full-fat yogurt
1 tablespoon lemon extract
1¼ cups whole milk
½ cup freshly squeezed lemon juice
1 tablespoon lemon zest

FOR THE BLACKBERRY SAUCE
2 cups blackberries
1 cup granulated sugar

1 teaspoon unflavored gelatin powder
2 tablespoons cold water

FOR THE GARNISH
½ recipe Almond Buttercream
  (page 130)
Edible gold leaf (optional)

Fresh basil leaves
½ cup blackberries

CONTINUED >

1. Preheat the oven to 325°F. Spray the pans with baking spray and set aside.

2. To make the cake: In a large bowl, combine the all-purpose flour, cake flour, baking soda, baking powder, and salt and whisk together.

3. In a different bowl, using a mixer, cream together the butter, sugar, olive oil, and vegetable oil on low speed.

4. Add the eggs one at a time, mix well, then add the yogurt, lemon extract, and milk. Mix on medium speed for 1 minute.

5. Add the lemon juice and zest to the wet mixture.

6. Sift in the dry ingredients, slowly at first. Mix on medium speed until the ingredients are well combined. Remember to scrape down the bowl with a spatula so that all ingredients get mixed evenly.

7. Distribute the batter evenly into the prepared pans. Bake for 20 to 25 minutes, or until a toothpick inserted into the center comes out clean.

8. While the cake is baking, make the blackberry sauce: In a saucepan, cook the blackberries and sugar over low heat, stirring occasionally. Cook for 7 to 8 minutes, until the sauce is rich in color.

9. Remove the blackberries from the heat and pour into a new bowl. Bloom the gelatin in cold water for 5 minutes.

10. Add the gelatin to the blackberries, stir well, and chill for 30 minutes.

11. Trim the edges off the cakes so they are straight and even. Cut the cakes in half. You should have 4 even rectangles of cake. Cut the halves into thirds.

12. To decorate, pipe stars on the top of the cake with the almond buttercream you prepared beforehand. Use a spoon to place some of the blackberry sauce on the buttercream.

13. Stack another piece of cake on top of the layer of buttercream and blackberries. Use the round tip to pipe more almond buttercream on the top of the cake. Cover the cake. Top it off with a whole blackberry from the sauce.

14. Use tweezers to pull apart a small amount of gold leaf and place the flecks on top of the cake (if using). Garnish with basil and fresh blackberries. Continue with the remaining cakes, buttercream, blackberry sauce, and garnishes.

CHOCOLATE DECADENCE

EQUIPMENT NEEDED
2 (9-by-13-inch) pans
Palette knife
Cake scraper
1 small (12-inch) piping bag
4B piping tip
Cake board/drum

PREP TIME 15 minutes
BAKE TIME 30 to 35 minutes
DECORATING TIME 15 minutes
MAKES 1 (2-layer) sheet cake
SERVES 20 to 25

I love a good chocolate cake, and when it comes to making one for friends and family who also love it, I turn to this recipe. Using a combination of melted dark chocolate and dark cocoa powder, this flavorful cake goes beautifully with a rich buttercream and is even more enjoyable with a smooth ganache. You can decorate or top it with anything you'd like, from fresh berries to sprinkles for a more colorful look.

FOR THE CAKE
Nonstick baking spray
2½ cups all-purpose flour
1 teaspoon baking powder
1½ teaspoons baking soda
¼ cup dark cocoa powder
½ teaspoon salt
1 cup semisweet chocolate chunks

1¼ cups whole milk, divided
8 tablespoons (1 stick) salted
  butter, melted
½ cup vegetable oil
2 cups granulated sugar
3 large eggs
½ cup sour cream

FOR THE BUTTERCREAM
2 recipes Vanilla Buttercream
  (page 28)

¾ cup dark cocoa powder

FOR THE GANACHE
2 cups dark chocolate chips
1 cup heavy (whipping) cream

1 tablespoon salted butter, at room
  temperature

FOR TOPPING
½ cup blueberries
1½ cups strawberries

½ cup blackberries

CONTINUED >

1. Preheat the oven to 350°F. Line the pans with parchment paper, then spray with baking spray and set aside.

2. To make the cake: In a large bowl, whisk the flour, baking powder, baking soda, cocoa powder, and salt. Set aside.

3. In a heat-safe container, microwave the chocolate and ¼ cup of milk in 20-second increments, until melted.

4. In another bowl, combine the butter, oil, and sugar. Pour in the chocolate mixture.

5. Add the eggs one at a time, mixing between each addition.

6. Stir in the sour cream and mix well.

7. Add in the remaining 1 cup of milk and combine well.

8. Sift in the dry ingredients a little at a time. Mix everything together for about 1 minute with a whisk.

9. Divide the batter evenly between the pans and bake for 30 to 35 minutes, or until a toothpick inserted in the center comes out clean.

10. When they are cooled, trim the edges of the cake. You should have two equally sized portions of sheet cake. Wrap with plastic wrap and freeze for at least 20 minutes.

11. Prepare the chocolate buttercream: Combine the vanilla buttercream and the cocoa powder in a large bowl and fold together with a spatula.

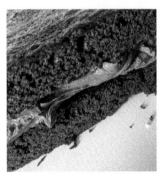

12. Spread a small amount of buttercream onto a cake board.

13. Place one layer of the cake onto the board and frost it with the buttercream. Stack the second layer on top and trim off some of the edges so that they are as straight as possible.

14. Use a palette knife or cake comb to crumb coat the cake with the chocolate buttercream. Chill in the refrigerator while you prepare the ganache.

15. To make the ganache: In a heat-safe bowl, microwave the chocolate and heavy cream for 1½ minutes.

16. Let stand for 1 minute and then stir with a whisk. Add the butter and whisk until a velvety texture is achieved. Let it stand while you frost the cake.

17. Spread 2½ cups of the chocolate buttercream onto the chilled cake. Cover the entirety of the cake. It won't look smooth at first; you just want it covered.

18. Use a scraper to drag along the sides and smooth them out.

19. Flatten the surface with a large palette knife.

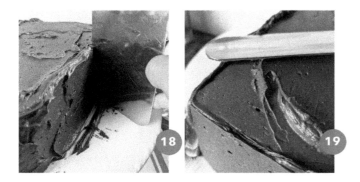

CONTINUED >

20. Scrape the sides again. The buttercream should push up and create a ridge around the edges.

21. Chill the cake for 20 minutes and trim the edges off with a sharp knife.

22. Pour the ganache onto the chilled cake. Spread it evenly over the top of the cake to the edges. The cake should have a drip naturally when you pour the ganache.

23. If you want to create more drips, add them with a spoon.

24. Fill a piping bag fitted with a 4B tip with the rest of the buttercream and pipe a border around the bottom of the cake. Chill the cake for 20 minutes. When the cake is chilled, remove from the refrigerator. Place the berries directly onto the ganache, spreading them out a bit (you want them to appear vertical). Alternatively, you can use sprinkles in place of the berries.

Once you have gotten the hang of baking cakes and frosting them in basic ways—as we did with sheet cakes—you may want to explore the world of bespoke layered cakes. As we move into decorating layered cakes, I will share my favorite tips and tricks to help you discover your hidden talents as a cake artist.

All these recipes, not including the buttercream, can be made in a large bowl using a whisk. Have an electric mixer prepared to make the buttercream. These are some of my favorite beautiful and fun layered cake tutorials to help you on your baking journey. Soon you will be creating one-tier beauties!

LAYER CAKES

RED VELVET CAKE

EQUIPMENT NEEDED
3 (9-inch) round pans
Palette knife
Cake drum/board (optional)

PREP TIME 15 minutes
BAKE TIME 25 to 30 minutes
DECORATING TIME 10 minutes
MAKES 1 (3-layer, 9-inch) round cake
SERVES 10 to 15

Soft, fluffy red velvet cake with rich cream cheese frosting is here served with layers exposed and decorated with a crown of edible flowers. This classic cake originating in the American South is great for a beginning cake decorator, as it requires only basic skills to make a beautiful and crowd-pleasing cake. Red velvet somehow always takes center stage on the table.

Nonstick baking spray
8 tablespoons (1 stick) salted
  butter, melted
½ cup vegetable oil
2 cups granulated sugar
3 large eggs
1 cup sour cream, at room
  temperature
1 cup whole milk, at room temperature
1 tablespoon cocoa powder

3 tablespoons hot water
1½ teaspoons vanilla extract
1 cup all-purpose flour
1¾ cups cake flour
1 teaspoon baking powder
1½ teaspoons baking soda
3 tablespoons red food coloring
1 teaspoon white vinegar
Package edible flowers

FOR THE CREAM CHEESE FROSTING
1½ cups (3 sticks) salted butter, at
  room temperature
4 ounces cream cheese, at room
  temperature

1 teaspoon vanilla extract
4 cups confectioners' sugar, sifted

CONTINUED >

1. Preheat the oven to 325°F. Spray the pans with baking spray and set aside.

2. In a large bowl, mix together the butter, oil, and sugar until well combined.

3. Add the eggs one at a time, mixing well after each addition.

4. Mix in the sour cream first and then the milk. Dissolve the cocoa powder in the hot water. Add the cocoa powder mixture and vanilla to the wet mixture and whisk until combined.

5. Combine the all-purpose flour, cake flour, baking powder, and baking soda and sift into the wet mixture.

6. Add in the red food coloring and vinegar and mix well for 1 to 2 minutes.

7. Divide the batter evenly among the three prepared pans. Bake for 25 to 30 minutes, or until a toothpick inserted in the center comes out clean.

8. After removing the cakes from the oven, let them cool on a wire rack.

9. To make the cream cheese frosting: Using a mixer, beat the butter and cream cheese until fluffy. Add in the vanilla, and then slowly add the confectioners' sugar.

10. Spread a bit of the frosting onto the cake board or a plate and press one cooled layer onto the surface so that it sticks.

11. Using a large spatula, spread a third of the buttercream onto the cake. Don't be afraid to let it drop over the sides—you'll be going for an overfilled look.

12. Lay the second layer over the buttercream and repeat step 11. Place the last layer on top and press down slightly on the center to level it.

13. Spread the rest of the buttercream over the top of the cake, and this time do not let it spill over the edges.

14. Use a large palette knife and turntable to carve a spiral in the frosting by rotating the turntable and pressing down on the surface with tip of the palette knife.

15. Place edible flowers around the edge of the top of the cake, if you like.

Make sure you use edible flowers; many stores carry seasonal hand-picked packages.

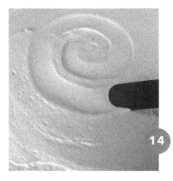

SPRINKLE PARTY CAKE

EQUIPMENT NEEDED
4 (6-inch) round pans
Cake board/drum
Palette knives (small and large)
Tall scraper
4 piping bags
3 1A (round) and
  1M piping tip
Gel food coloring

PREP TIME 15 minutes
BAKE TIME 30 to 35 minutes
DECORATING TIME 1 hour
MAKES 1 (4-layer, 6-inch) round cake
SERVES 15 to 20

This vanilla cake filled with rainbow sprinkles and sandwiched with multicolor frosting is covered in white buttercream and finished with a colorful sprinkle fade for a beautiful presentation. This cake is best served at room temperature, so take it out of the refrigerator 1 to 2 hours before serving.

Nonstick baking spray
8 tablespoons (1 stick) salted
  butter, melted
½ cup vegetable oil
2 cups granulated sugar
3 large eggs, at room temperature
2 teaspoons vanilla extract
1 cup plain full-fat yogurt, at room
  temperature
1 cup whole milk, at room temperature

1½ cups all-purpose flour, sifted
1¾ cups cake flour
1½ teaspoons baking soda
1 teaspoon baking powder
½ teaspoon salt
⅔ cup rainbow sprinkles
Simple syrup (pages 12–13)
¼ to ½ cup colorful sprinkle medley of
  choice, for decorating
Vegetable shortening

FOR THE BUTTERCREAM
3½ cups (7 sticks) salted butter, at
  room temperature
2 teaspoons vanilla extract

½ teaspoon salt
6½ cups confectioners' sugar, sifted

1. Preheat the oven to 325°F. Spray the pans with baking spray and set aside.

2. In a large bowl, mix together the butter, oil, and sugar until well combined, then incorporate the eggs one at a time, mixing after each addition.

CONTINUED >

3. Add in the vanilla, yogurt, and milk and mix until smooth. Then, slowly add the sifted all-purpose flour, cake flour, baking soda, baking powder, and salt.

4. Mix well for 1 minute; the batter should be slightly runny and thick.

5. Fold in the sprinkles, making sure they are distributed throughout the batter.

6. Divide the batter evenly into the prepared pans. Bake for 30 to 35 minutes, or until a toothpick inserted in the center comes out clean.

7. Level or tort the cakes while they are still warm and brush with the simple syrup. Wrap up and freeze.

As discussed in chapter 3, working with frozen layers makes it easier to do the stacking and crumb-coating processes.

8. To make the buttercream: In a mixer, beat the butter on medium speed for 2 minutes. Add the vanilla and salt.

9. Scrape down the sides so that all the ingredients are well combined. Add the confectioners' sugar in small batches.

10. After adding all the confectioners' sugar, beat on medium speed for 1 to 2 minutes, until smooth and fluffy.

11. Using a measuring cup, scoop 1 cup of frosting into each of three bowls.

12. Color each bowl of buttercream a different color of your choice, using 3 to 5 drops, or as many as it takes to get your desired color.

13. To start stacking the layers, spread a bit of buttercream on the board, which should be placed on a turntable. Place one frozen layer on the board, center it, and press down firmly so that the buttercream hardens and sticks to it.

14. Fill a piping bag with a 1A (or equivalent) round tip with one color of buttercream and make a large swirl on the layer.

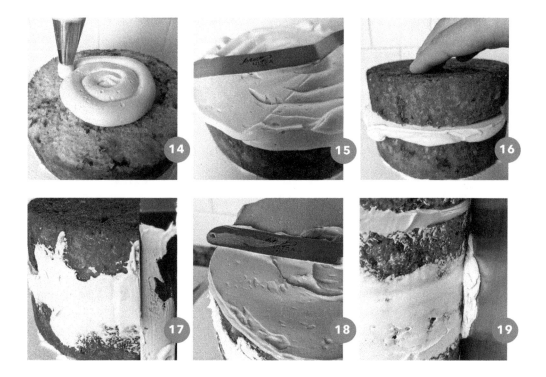

15. Use a small offset spatula to spread the buttercream and level it while you rotate the turntable.

16. Place the second layer over the first one, cut-side down, making sure it is centered. Press down slightly to get rid of any air gaps between the cake and the buttercream.

17. As you rotate the turntable, use a scraper to smooth the sides and clean up any buttercream that has gone over the edges.

18. Repeat steps 14 to 17 for the next layer, using a different color buttercream.

19. After you are done spreading the last layer of colored buttercream, invert the last cake layer so that the bottom is on top.

20. Use a tall scraper to clean the sides of the cake and fill in any gaps of buttercream.

21. Use a small amount of the white buttercream to crumb coat the cake.

CONTINUED >

22. Scoop the white buttercream on top of the cake. Use a large palette knife to spread the buttercream down the sides and evenly onto the cake.

23. Smooth the top by rotating the table toward you as you push the palette knife away, creating a flat surface. Then use a tall scraper to smooth the sides, scraping at a 45-degree angle against the cake as you rotate the turntable toward the scraper. The trick is to keep scraping away a little at a time until you're satisfied. Chill for 10 minutes.

24. When chilled, fill in any visible holes by patching them up with a small palette knife. Go over the sides with the tall scraper again. You may have to scrape a few times before the patches are no longer visible.

25. Let the cake chill for another 10 to 15 minutes, then take a sharp knife and run it under hot water. At a 180-degree angle, cut the edge of the cake off.

26. Use a small offset spatula to very lightly swipe the edges toward the cake (sweep the spatula toward you, not away).

27. Fill a piping bag fitted with the 1M tip with the rest of the white buttercream and pipe tall swirls to border the cake. The swirls should be close enough to each other so that there are no gaps between them.

28. Prepare the sprinkles by separating the larger ones from the smaller ones.

29. Rub a bit of shortening onto your gloved fingers. You only want a very thin layer. Dip your greased fingertip into the smaller sprinkles and apply them onto the cold cake. Apply mostly at the bottom, and less toward the top for the ombre effect.

30. Apply the larger sprinkles, with most toward the bottom and fewer toward the top.

COOKIES AND CRÈME

EQUIPMENT NEEDED
4 (6-inch) round pans
Cake drum/board
Turntable
3 large piping bags
1A or 2A (round), 124 or 125 (ruffle),
  and 1M piping tips
Short cake scraper
Palette knives (large and small)

PREP TIME 15 minutes
BAKE TIME 25 to 30 minutes
DECORATING TIME 1 hour
MAKES 1 (4-layer, 6-inch) round cake
SERVES 15 to 20

Layers of chocolate cake and Oreo buttercream are wrapped up with exposed cookies to result in a bold appearance. This cake is great for a beginning cake decorator. It requires only basic skills to make a beautiful cake that takes center stage on the table.

Nonstick baking spray
8 tablespoons (1 stick) salted
  butter, melted
½ cup vegetable oil
1¾ cups granulated sugar
½ cup cocoa powder
3 large eggs, at room temperature

1 cup sour cream, at room temperature
1 cup whole milk, at room temperature
2½ cups all-purpose flour
1 teaspoon baking powder
1 teaspoon baking soda
½ teaspoon salt
Simple syrup (pages 12–13)

FOR THE BUTTERCREAM
10 Oreo cookies, filling removed
1 recipe Swiss Meringue Buttercream
  (page 29)

½ recipe Vanilla Buttercream (page 28)

FOR DECORATING
6 Oreos, broken into quarters,
  filling removed

8 whole Oreo cookies

1. Preheat the oven to 350°F. Spray the pans with baking spray and set aside.

2. Mix the butter, oil, and sugar well for about 1 minute.

3. Add in the cocoa powder and the eggs one at a time, mixing after each addition. Mix in the sour cream and milk.

CONTINUED >

4. Combine the flour, baking powder, baking soda, and salt in a large bowl, whisk for 20 seconds, then sift into the wet mixture.

5. Divide the batter evenly into the prepared pans and bake for 25 to 30 minutes, or until a toothpick inserted into the center comes out clean.

6. Level or tort the cake layers while they are still warm. Brush with the simple syrup, wrap, and freeze for 2 to 3 hours.

7. To make the buttercream: Using a food processor, grind the Oreo cookies into a fine powder. If you do not have a processor, use a zip-top bag and heavy rolling pin to crush the cookies into a powder.

8. Mix the prepared buttercreams together, then fold the powdered Oreo cookies into the frosting.

9. Apply the first cake layer to the board. Fill a large piping bag fitted with the round tip with half of the buttercream and pipe a layer of frosting onto the cake.

10. Set the next layer on top the buttercream and repeat step 9.

11. After all layers have been stacked, scrape the excess frosting off with the cake scraper and proceed to crumb coat the cake. Chill for 30 minutes.

12. Using the small palette knife, apply a thin layer of the buttercream around the middle of the cake.

13. Place the Oreo quarters on the buttercream layer that you applied.

14. Fill another piping bag fitted with the ruffle tip with half of the remaining buttercream and, starting from the bottom, pipe around the cake and up toward the Oreos. The stopping point should be just over the bottom of the Oreos.

15. Next, pipe around the cake over the top line of the Oreos. Continue piping buttercream until you cover the top.

16. Use a small palette knife to level and flatten the top. Use the short scraper to smooth the sides of the bottom portion of buttercream.

17. Repeat the same process with the top portion of buttercream. When you are satisfied with the smoothness, chill the cake for 10 minutes.

18. After you have chilled the cake, patch up any rough spots in the buttercream with a small palette knife and leftover buttercream. Repeat the scraping process over the patched buttercream to achieve smooth sides. The result should be smooth cake sides revealing the broken Oreo pieces.

19. Chill the cake for another 10 minutes, then cut off the edges with a sharp, wet knife.

CONTINUED >

20. Use a sharp knife to mark 4 slight guidelines on the cake (think of cutting a pie into 8 pieces). Place a whole Oreo on the edge of the cake on a guideline.

21. Fill a piping bag fitted with the 1M tip with the rest of the buttercream and pipe a tall swirl next to the Oreo. Repeat until the top of the cake has a completed border of swirls and cookies.

VANILLA DE LECHE

EQUIPMENT NEEDED
3 (6-inch) round pans
Cake drum/board
Turntable
Palette knives (large and small)
Cake scraper
6 piping bags
1A, 1M, 8B, 4B, 223, and
  352 piping tips
Oil-based food coloring (4 to 5 colors)

PREP TIME 15 minutes
BAKE TIME 35 minutes
DECORATING TIME 1 hour
MAKES 1 (3-layer, 6-inch round) cake
SERVES 8 to 12

This classic vanilla cake is filled with a delicious dulce de leche buttercream and covered in Swiss meringue buttercream and elegant floral piping. The color palette on this can easily be changed to your preferences. This recipe allows you to be creative with your choices of colors and experiment with different ways to pipe with flourish.

Nonstick baking spray
1 cup all-purpose flour
2 teaspoons baking soda
1 teaspoon baking powder
½ teaspoon salt
8 tablespoons (1 stick) salted
  butter, melted
¾ cup vegetable oil

2½ cups granulated sugar
1 large egg, at room temperature
½ cup plain full-fat yogurt, at room
  temperature
1 cup whole milk, at room temperature
2 vanilla pods or 2 teaspoons
  vanilla extract

FOR THE DULCE DE LECHE BUTTERCREAM
1½ cups (3 sticks) salted butter, at
  room temperature
½ cup canned dulce de leche
½ teaspoon salt

4 cups confectioners' sugar, sifted
1 recipe Swiss Meringue Buttercream
  (page 29)

FOR DECORATING
1 recipe Swiss Meringue Buttercream
  (page 29)

Dragées or other sprinkles

CONTINUED >

1. Preheat the oven to 350°F. Spray the pans with baking spray and set aside.

2. In a large bowl, combine the flour, baking soda, baking powder, and salt and whisk for 30 seconds, then sift into another large bowl.

3. Using a mixer, cream the butter, oil, and sugar together on medium speed for 1 minute.

4. Whisk the egg, then add the yogurt and milk. Whisk well for 1 minute.

5. If you are using vanilla pods, slice the pods open down the middle. Scrape out the vanilla seeds with the end of a utensil or edge of a spoon. Add them to the wet mixture. If you are using vanilla extract, add that now.

6. Add in the dry ingredients a little at a time and whisk well, but do not overbeat. The batter should be smooth and slightly thick.

7. Divide the batter evenly into the prepared pans and bake for 20 minutes, then lower to 325°F and bake for 15 minutes. Level, wrap, and freeze for 1 hour.

8. To make the dulce de leche buttercream: Creaming the butter and dulce de leche together, slowly add the salt and sifted confectioners' sugar. Place the buttercream into a bag fitted with a 1A piping tip.

9. Spread a small amount of the buttercream onto the cake board. Stick the first frozen layer of cake onto the board, making sure that it is centered. Press down somewhat firmly to level it.

10. Take the bag filled with the dulce de leche buttercream and swirl it onto the cake. The layer should look even and fill the entire surface of the cake.

11. Continue alternating layers of cake and buttercream, with the last layer inverted so that the bottom is on top. Scrape away any excess buttercream.

12. You may choose to chill before crumb coating or go straight to crumb coating at this point. After you have crumb coated the cake, chill it for 30 minutes.

13. Measure the Swiss meringue buttercream into 2 (1-cup) portions, 2 (½-cup) portions, and 1 (½-cup) portion. Color the portions of buttercream you separated with 3 to 5 drops of the food coloring and coordinate them with the following tips: 1 cup—1M, 1 cup—8B, ½ cup—4B, ½ cup—223, and ¼ cup—352. Mix the remainder of the buttercream in the color of your choice.

CONTINUED >

14. Use a large palette knife to apply the large batch of colored buttercream to the cake for its final coat.

15. Use a tall scraper to scrape to smooth the sides. When you are satisfied with the smoothness, chill the cake for 15 minutes.

16. Use a sharp, wet knife to cut the edges off the top of the cake.

17. Use the 1M color to pipe a small swirl on the edge of the top.

18. Pipe a rosette on the top edge of the cake onto the swirl, which will act as a support; it should look like the rosette is floating on the edge. Pipe a few more around the edge in the same manner.

19. Pipe a few rosettes around the bottom as well, leaving some space between them.

20. Use the 8B color to pipe large stars next to the rosettes; remember to pipe randomly.

21. The cake should look like it has two crowns, one on top and one on the bottom. Gaps are okay and will be filled.

22. Use the 4B color to pipe smaller stars to fill some of the gaps.

23. Fill in smaller gaps with the 223 color. They should look like tiny flower accents.

24. Pipe the leaf accents with the 352 color. Pipe randomly and fill in any remaining gaps.

25. Place dragées or other sprinkles on the piped areas as a finishing touch.

Dragées are small confectionary encased in a hard outer shell. In the cake-decorating world, they are often pearl- or metallic-covered pieces of sugar.

HEY PUMPKIN! SPICED CAKE

EQUIPMENT NEEDED
4 (6-inch) round pans
Cake drum/board
Turntable
Palette knives
Tall cake scraper
5 piping bags
(2) 1M, 8B, 2 or 3, and 199 piping tips
Gel food coloring (4 to 5 colors)

PREP TIME 15 minutes
BAKE TIME 30 to 35 minutes
DECORATING TIME 1 hour 30 minutes,
  plus 1–2 hours for freezing
MAKES 1 (4-layer, 6-inch) round cake
SERVES 15 to 20

This fun holiday number features four layers of spiced pumpkin cake with cream cheese frosting. A bold base coat is decorated with colorful pumpkins made with basic piping tips. By now you should be familiar with the entire process of decorating. This cake is a great way to practice the skills that you have learned from the previous chapters.

FOR THE CAKE

Nonstick baking spray
1 cup vegetable oil
8 tablespoons (1 stick) salted
  butter, melted
2½ cups brown sugar, packed
1 cup granulated sugar
1 large egg
1 (15-ounce) can pure pumpkin puree
4 tablespoons honey

1 cup plain full-fat yogurt, at room
  temperature
1½ cups whole milk, at room
  temperature
2 cups all-purpose flour
3 teaspoons baking soda
2 teaspoons ground cinnamon
½ teaspoon ground nutmeg
½ teaspoon salt
Simple syrup (pages 12–13)

FOR THE FILLING

Cream Cheese Frosting (page 32)

FOR THE VANILLA BUTTERCREAM

2 cups (4 sticks) salted butter, at room
  temperature

1 teaspoon vanilla extract
5½ cups confectioners' sugar, sifted

FOR DECORATING

Pretzels (twists or sticks, your choice)

CONTINUED >

1. Preheat the oven to 350°F. Spray the pans with baking spray and set aside.

2. To make the cake: Mix the oil, butter, brown sugar, and granulated sugar together well.

3. Add the egg, pumpkin puree, and honey and combine well. Then, add the yogurt and milk and whisk for 1 minute until incorporated.

4. In a large bowl, whisk the flour, baking soda, cinnamon, nutmeg, and salt for about 30 seconds.

5. Sift a third of the dry ingredients into the bowl of wet ingredients. Whisk well, then add the second third, whisk again, and add the rest.

6. The batter should be nice and thick. Divide it evenly into the prepared pans. Bake for 30 to 35 minutes, or until a toothpick inserted in the center comes out clean.

7. Level the cakes while they are still warm. Brush with the simple syrup, wrap, and freeze for 1 to 2 hours.

8. Fill the cake with the cream cheese frosting. Make the vanilla buttercream and use some of it to crumb coat the cake after you have filled and stacked it.

9. Color 3½ cups of the buttercream with 5 to 8 drops of food coloring in a bold hue.

10. Apply a final coat of colored buttercream to the cake. Remember, this process takes a few extra scrapes and trips to the refrigerator. When you are satisfied, chill and cut the uneven edges of the top of the cake off.

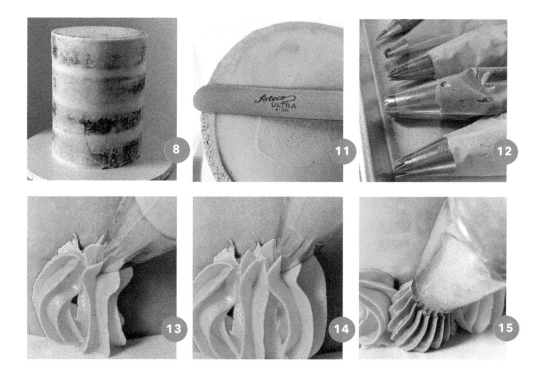

11. Using a light touch, sweep the remaining edges of the frosting toward the center of the cake with a small palette knife to create a nice flat surface.

12. Separate the remaining buttercream into the following parts: 1 cup, 1 cup, ½ cup, ½ cup, ¼ cup. Color each part with 5 to 8 drops of a different food coloring and fill the piping bags fitted with the tips listed in the equipment list. Remember, be comfortable using your own color choices!

13. Use a 1M tip to pipe a curved shape like a pumpkin on the bottom of the cake. Next, pipe a straight line up the middle.

14. Finish the pumpkin by piping another curved shape. It should look a little round. Pipe more of these pumpkins around the bottom, with some gaps between them.

15. Use the 8B to pipe larger pumpkins; they should be stars that are puffy and round. To achieve this, hold the tip a few centimeters from where you want it to land, squeeze, and release.

CONTINUED >

16. Use the 199 tip to fill in small gaps between the larger pieces that you piped.

17. Break the pretzels into stem lengths and place them on top of the pumpkins, including the 8B shapes.

18. Use the other 1M to pipe a few swirls on top of the cake. Pipe as many as you'd like.

19. On a small piece of parchment paper, make a pumpkin a with a 1M tip and freeze it.

20. When it has frozen, place it on top of the cake against a swirl. It should stand upright.

21. Use the small (2 or 3) round tip to pipe vines around the stems of the pumpkins.

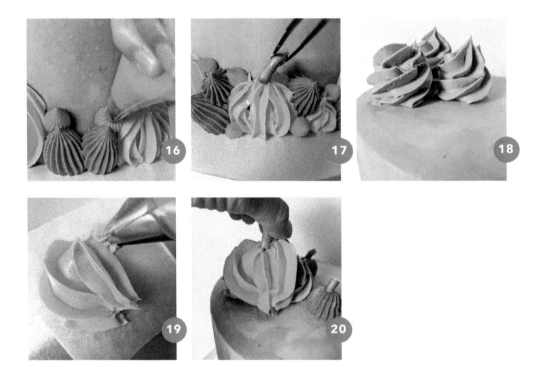

CHAI CHIC

EQUIPMENT NEEDED
4 (6-inch) round pans
Cake drum/board
Turntable
Tall cake scraper
Palette knives (large and small)
1 piping bag
2D piping tip
Gel food coloring (4 to 5 colors)
10 to 12 spray roses, de-stemmed

PREP TIME 15 minutes
BAKE TIME 30 to 35 minutes
DECORATING TIME 1 hour
MAKES 1 (4-layer, 6-inch) round cake
SERVES 15 to 20

Chai-flavored cake is wrapped in a beautiful coat of fuchsia buttercream for this stunning presentation. A navy drip falls down the sides of the cake and complements a color palette painted on with a spatula. A crown of fresh flowers completes the look of this chic beauty. This design is fully customizable from the buttercream and drip colors to the fresh flowers.

Nonstick baking spray
1½ cups vegetable oil
3 cups granulated sugar, plus
 4 tablespoons
2 eggs
4 cups all-purpose flour
1½ teaspoons chai spice

2 teaspoons baking soda
½ teaspoon salt
3 tablespoons honey mixed into
 1¾ cups whole milk, at room
 temperature
1 chai tea bag
¼ cup hot water

FOR THE HONEY BUTTERCREAM
1 recipe Vanilla Buttercream (page 28)
1½ cups (3 sticks) salted butter, at
 room temperature

3 tablespoons honey
½ teaspoon salt
4½ cups confectioners' sugar, sifted

FOR THE DRIP
⅓ cup white chocolate chips
3 tablespoons heavy (whipping) cream

Large metallic sprinkles
Oil-based coloring of your choice

CONTINUED >

1. Preheat the oven to 350°F. Spray the pans with baking spray and set aside.

2. Whisk together the oil and 3 cups of sugar for about 1 minute. Add in the eggs one at a time and whisk well.

3. In a large bowl, combine the flour, chai spice, baking soda, and salt and whisk together. Set aside.

4. Add half of the honey-milk mixture to the wet ingredients and combine well.

5. Sift half of the dry ingredients into the wet mixture and mix well for about 1 minute. The batter should be somewhat smooth and a little runny.

6. Repeat steps 4 to 5 with the last half of the ingredients. The batter should be smooth and slightly thick.

7. Divide the batter evenly into the prepared pans. Bake for 30 to 35 minutes, or until a toothpick inserted into the center comes out clean.

8. Prepare tea simple syrup by steeping the chai tea bag in the hot water for 5 minutes. Dissolve the remaining 4 tablespoons of sugar in the hot tea. Optional: Add a few drops of milk or cream to the tea solution.

9. Brush the tea solution onto the warm cake layer. Wrap and freeze for 1 to 2 hours.

10. Prepare the honey buttercream while waiting for the layers to freeze.

11. Fill and stack the cake layers with the honey buttercream. Chill for 15 minutes and then crumb coat. Take ¼ cup of the vanilla buttercream and set it aside. Color the larger portion of buttercream.

12. Apply the final coat of buttercream to the cake with a large spatula. Scrape a few times and then do patchwork on any holes or rough spots. If you are using a metal scraper, you may run it under hot water and use it to scrape the last few times, but only when you are sure it is your final go at scraping.

If you heat the comb too early in the scraping process, bubbles will appear on the buttercream.

13. To make the drip, microwave the white chocolate and cream in a microwave-safe container on high for 45 seconds. Stir it until it is smooth, then add 5 to 7 drops of the oil-based color of your choice.

14. Mix it slowly to make sure it is well combined. Set it aside for 30 minutes and chill the cake while you wait. Use a wet knife to neatly trim the edges off the top of the cake 10 minutes into chilling time.

15. After 30 minutes, use a spoon to pour the drip over the edge and let it drip down the sides, while turning the cake around.

You may practice your drips on the rim of a cup or bowl beforehand.

CONTINUED >

16. Spoon a small amount of drip onto the center of cake. Spread the drip with a small offset spatula while rotating the turntable. When you are satisfied with the top of the cake, chill it for 20 to 30 minutes.

17. Fill a piping bag fitted with the 2D tip with the remainder of the buttercream you used for the final coat. Pipe rosettes as a border around the top of the cake. The rosettes should be piped neatly next to each other.

It is important to let the drip chill and set otherwise, the rosettes will push the drip further down the sides.

18. Divide the vanilla buttercream you set aside earlier into three parts and make them three different colors.

19. Use a small offset spatula to paint a streak of buttercream on the bottom of the cake. Paint the streak upward as in the photo below.

20. Continue these streaks around the cake and leave gaps between them.

21. Take the second color and fill in the gaps this time, while continuing to streak the buttercream upward. Repeat the streaks around the cake, also leaving some gaps.

22. Do the same streaking process with the third color; this time you may streak in any direction. The result is a minimal amount of texture that is also eye-catching.

23. Before serving, place fresh flowers on the border of the cake. Place metallic sprinkles along the bottom and top border of the cake.

You may wrap the flowers (see page 139) or make sure they are completely edible and well washed.

Tiered cakes are often romanticized and linked to special occasions like weddings and anniversaries but are becoming more common for birthdays and other celebrations. They carry a look of prestige and craftmanship and require some extra attention like using dowels and plates.

You will learn how to stack a two- and three-tier cake in this chapter, as well as how to properly prepare flowers for decorating. We'll also build on the skills you have learned.

3D/SCULPTURAL AND
TIERED CAKES

RETRO LOVE CAKE

EQUIPMENT NEEDED
2 (6-inch) heart pans
Cake board/drum
Turntable
Palette knife
4 (4-by-12-inch) piping bags
1M, 6B, 4B, and 199 piping tips
Oil-based food coloring (4 to 6 drops
  each for bolder colors, 2 to 3 drops
  for pastel colors)

Cake scraper 3–5 tablespoons colorful
  sprinkles

PREP TIME 20 minutes
BAKE TIME 20 to 25 minutes
DECORATING TIME 30 minutes
MAKES 1 (2-layer, 6-inch) heart cake
SERVES 6 to 8

An easy-to-do vintage style piping known as Lambeth will win you over while making this cake. Filled with cookie dough buttercream and a warm brown-sugar sponge, this makes the perfect romantic cake to gift someone special. Lambeth-style borders are all about layering them in a horizontal fashion, and this tutorial will guide you through the basics of vintage piping on a fun heart shape.

FOR THE CAKE
Nonstick baking spray
4 tablespoons (½ stick) salted
  butter, melted
½ cup vegetable oil
½ cup packed brown sugar
½ cup granulated sugar
1 large egg, at room temperature

½ cup whole milk, at room
  temperature
1 teaspoon vanilla extract
1½ cups all-purpose flour
1 teaspoon baking soda
Pinch salt

FOR THE COOKIE DOUGH BUTTERCREAM
¼ cup all-purpose flour
1½ cups (3 sticks) salted butter, at
  room temperature
½ cup packed brown sugar
1 cup confectioners' sugar, sifted

½ teaspoon vanilla extract
Pinch salt
½ cup chocolate chips (milk, dark,
  white, your choice)

FOR DECORATING
1 recipe Swiss Meringue Buttercream
  (page 29)

4–5 maraschino cherries
3–5 tablespoons sprinkle medley

CONTINUED >

1. Preheat the oven to 350°F. Spray the pans with baking spray and set aside.

2. In a large bowl, combine the butter, oil, brown sugar, and granulated sugar. Mix well.

3. Beat in the egg and make sure it is incorporated. Add in the milk and vanilla.

4. In a separate bowl, whisk the flour, baking soda, and salt. Sift the dry ingredients into the bowl of wet ingredients and combine thoroughly.

5. Divide the batter evenly into the pans and bake for 20 to 25 minutes, or until a toothpick inserted in the center comes out clean. While warm, prepare the cakes for stacking by leveling, wrapping, and freezing.

6. Make the cookie dough buttercream: Heat treat the flour by spreading it onto a parchment paper–lined small baking sheet and cook at 350°F for 5 minutes. Cream the butter on medium speed for 2 minutes until light and fluffy. Gradually add the brown sugar, then the confectioners' sugar, and finally the vanilla and salt. Beat for 2 minutes on medium speed and fold in chocolate chips.

7. Fill the cake with all of the cookie dough buttercream. Fill in any gaps in the layer of buttercream and scrape the sides after you have filled it.

8. Crumb coat the entire cake and refrigerate for 15 to 20 minutes.

9. To decorate: Color 2 cups of the Swiss meringue buttercream (ideally, you will want a lighter color than the others you will make). Frost the cake with the colored buttercream. Save whatever extra buttercream scrapes off in a small bowl.

10. Use the palette knife to smooth the top and flatten it as you would with a round cake by rotating the turntable.

11. Scrape the sides smooth. Go along with the shape of the heart and the buttercream will push out naturally, so long as you scrape evenly.

12. Chill the cake for 10 to 15 minutes, then cut the edges of the top off with a sharp knife.

13. Divide the rest of the buttercream into 1½ cups, 1 cup, and 2 (½-cup) portions. Color them and put them into the piping bags with tips fitted in them.

14. Use the 1M to pipe a border around the bottom of the cake. Pipe another border on the top of the cake, slightly off the edge of the cake. You should have two borders that align with one another.

15. Use the 6B to pipe a border on top of the bottom 1M border. Use the 4B to pipe a border on top of the 6B one. Use the 199 to pipe a border under the 1M one on the top.

16. The best part is getting to fill the entire top of the cake with a pretty sprinkle medley. Use one that matches the colors on the cake! Place the maraschino cherries around the top border to make it look extra vintage.

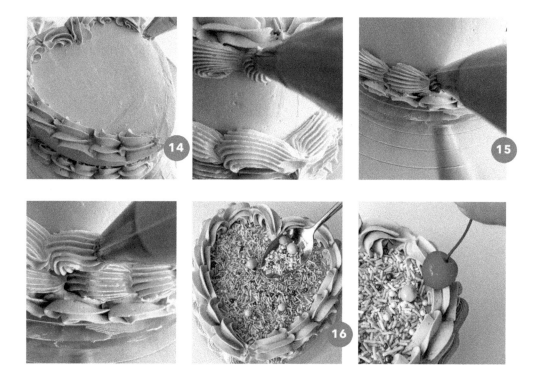

PASTEL WINTER WONDERLAND

EQUIPMENT NEEDED

4 (6-inch) round pans

1 (9-inch) round pan

Cake board/drum

Turntable

Palette knives (large and small)

Oil-based and gel-based food
 coloring (2 to 4 drops of each
 color used)

Fondant roller

X-Acto knife or sharp blade equivalent

Edible glue

Paintbrush

4 piping bags

352, 18, 104, and 1M piping tips

Lollipop sticks

Small tray

PREP TIME 45 minutes

BAKE TIME 30 to 35 minutes

DECORATING TIME 1 hour

MAKES 1 (4-layer, 6-inch) round cake

SERVES 10 to 15

When I think of winter, I think of cold, white, and gray weather, but when translating that to a cake, I also want to add some color and fun. With this Pastel Winter Wonderland you will learn how to use different mediums to create an eye-catching cake that boasts 3D elements and employs a variety of techniques for a stunning result. A refreshing peppermint buttercream is the perfect partner for a spongy and delicious white chocolate cake. The cake is then wrapped up in a wintery grayish-blue buttercream and adorned with hand-piped pastel trees.

FOR THE CAKE

2 recipes Chocolate Decadence Cake
 (page 75) replacing the regular
 chocolate with white chocolate chips
 and leaving out the cocoa powder
 and 1 egg

Sugar cones

1 large marshmallow (optional)

Vegetable shortening

Large metallic sprinkles

1 to 2 teaspoons sprinkle medley

FOR THE PEPPERMINT BUTTERCREAM

½ candy cane

1½ cups (3 sticks) salted butter, at
 room temperature

1 cup white chocolate chips, melted
 then cooled at room temperature for
 5 minutes

4 cups confectioners' sugar

1 teaspoon peppermint extract

CONTINUED >

FOR THE VANILLA BUTTERCREAM

3 cups (6 sticks) salted butter, at room temperature

6½ cups confectioners' sugar, sifted

1½ teaspoons vanilla extract

½ teaspoon salt

1 to 2 tablespoons heavy (whipping) cream

FOR THE FONDANT MOUNTAIN

1 cup mini marshmallows

1 tablespoon salted butter

1 cup crisped rice cereal

1 baseball-size ball fondant

1. Follow the recipe for the Chocolate Decadence Cake. Bake and prepare the layers for filling and stacking. This includes leveling/torting, brushing with a simple syrup, wrapping, and freezing. You should have 4 (6-inch) rounds and 1 (9-inch) round. The latter will be extra; save it for other cake-related treats.

2. Make the peppermint buttercream: Put the candy cane in a plastic bag and use a heavy rolling pin to smash the candy into fine pieces.

3. Cream the butter on medium speed for a few minutes until fluffy. Gradually add the melted white chocolate. Sift in the confectioners' sugar. Fold in the crushed candy cane and peppermint extract. Fill and stack the cake layers with the peppermint buttercream. Crumb coat and chill for 30 minutes.

4. Make the vanilla buttercream: Cream the butter on medium for about 2 minutes. Add in the confectioners' sugar a little at a time, followed by the vanilla, salt, and heavy cream. Separate 3 cups of the buttercream into a large bowl and color it with 4 or 5 drops of oil-based food coloring. This will be the base coat.

5. Frost the cake with the colored frosting you've prepared and scrape until the sides are smooth. Cutting the edge of the top of the cake off is always optional and in this case, I eventually cut it off for a nice sharp edge. Chill in the refrigerator while you prepare the other components of the cake.

6. Make the fondant mountain: In a large microwave-safe container, microwave the mini marshmallows and the butter on high for 45 seconds. Stir in the rice cereal and mix well. Let cool for 30 minutes.

7. Use gloves to handle the cereal. Shape it into a mountain form with a little peak. You should have a chunky rice cereal mountain.

8. Color four-fifths of the fondant gray with gel food coloring and leave the rest white. Roll out the gray fondant to ⅛-inch thickness.

9. Gently cover the mountain you formed with the fondant. Trim off any excess.

10. Roll the remaining white fondant out to ⅛-inch thickness.

11. Using the X-Acto knife, cut out a wavy shape (like a cartoon thought bubble). Roll this shape out a bit to even it out.

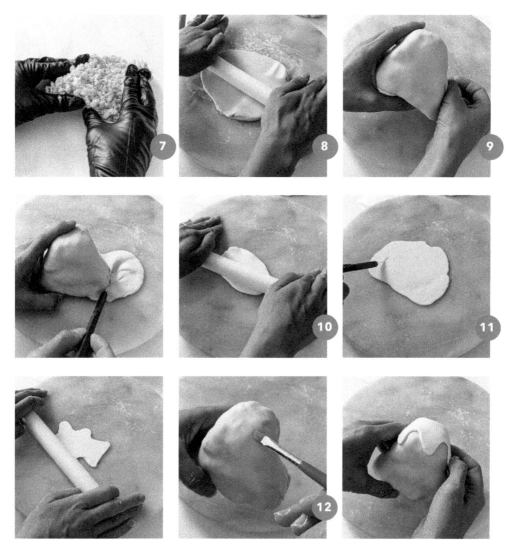

CONTINUED >

12. Place the white part on the peak first and adjust if necessary. It should simply look like snow on a mountain. If you are satisfied with the white fondant, apply some water or edible glue to the peak. Stick the snow fondant to the peak and smooth down the sides a bit.

13. Cut two sugar cones in half to make four halves. Do this by gently sawing a serrated knife down the center of each cone. It is very easy to break cones, so don't be discouraged. You will want to have some full ones to decorate as well, so make sure to have extras.

14. Divide the leftover buttercream into three parts and make them three different colors. Assign them to the appropriate piping bags and tips.

15. If you have a large marshmallow, place one on the lollipop stick and push it into the cone. This will help you rotate the cone as you pipe. You may also simply hold the tip of the cone.

16. Twirl the cone and pipe leaves pointing downward with the 352. Cover the entire cone with the leaf piping. Set it on a tray lined up.

17. Use the 18 to pipe stars onto another half cone. Set it on the tray.

18. On another cone, use the 104 to wiggle the tip and pipe some upward ruffles. Hold the cone sideways to do this.

19. Continue to pipe frosting onto as many cones as you like.

20. Spread some buttercream on top of the cake to act as a glue. Place the mountain on top of the buttercream you spread. Next, place a piped tree in the spot you desire. Use more buttercream to affix some trees to the bottom portion of the cake as well.

21. Take any leftover buttercream and place it in a piping bag fitted with a 1M tip. Pipe some random flourishes on the cake.

22. Use gloves and a bit of shortening to apply sprinkles onto the cake.

Play around with this design. Make the trees smaller by cutting the cones in half horizontally. The possibilities are endless!

"CUTE AS CAN BEE" HONEY-ALMOND CAKE

EQUIPMENT NEEDED

1 (8-cavity) silicone 4-inch cake mold

4 (6-inch) round cake pans

Cake board/drum

Turntable

Palette knives

Tall cake scraper

Yellow gel food coloring
 (5 drops yellow)

12-inch food-safe wooden dowel

Bee-related stencils

1 piping bag

8B (large star) piping tip or equivalent

Seasonal flowers

Scissors

Floral wire (24 or 26 gauge)

Floral tape

Small fondant rolling pin

X-Acto knife or sharp blade equivalent

1 sheet wafer paper

Jumbo/bubble tea straws

PREP TIME 30 minutes

BAKE TIME 30 to 35 minutes

DECORATING TIME 1 hour 30 minutes

MAKES 1 (2-tiered) cake, with a 6-inch
 round and 4-inch round

SERVES 15 to 20

Life is bee-utiful, have some cake! A honey-almond cake, in fact. A yellow ombre makes this a happy cake with a springtime feel, and the floating bees will be the stars of the show. For this one, you will want to make the bees ahead of time so that they have time to harden. You may use any cake recipe you like, so long as it yields 4 (6-inch) round cake layers and 7 or 8 (4-inch) layers. For the purposes of this tutorial, I have included the honey-almond cake recipe.

FOR THE CAKE

Nonstick baking spray

1 cup all-purpose flour

3½ cups cake flour

2 teaspoons baking soda

1 teaspoon baking powder

½ teaspoon salt

1 cup (2 sticks) salted butter, melted

1 cup vegetable oil

4 cups granulated sugar

2 large eggs, at room temperature

2 tablespoons almond extract

2 tablespoons honey

1 cup plain full-fat yogurt, at room
 temperature

1½ cups whole milk, at room
 temperature

Simple syrup (pages 12–13)

CONTINUED >

FOR THE ALMOND BUTTERCREAM

2 cups (4 sticks) salted butter, at room
  temperature
5¾ cups confectioners' sugar, sifted
2 teaspoons almond extract

½ teaspoon salt
1 to 2 tablespoons heavy
  (whipping) cream

FOR DECORATING

1 recipe Swiss Meringue Buttercream
  (page 29)
1 tennis ball–size ball fondant

Edible gold leaf sheets

1. Preheat the oven to 350°F. Spray the molds and pans with baking spray and
    set aside.

2. Make the cake: In a large bowl, whisk together the all-purpose flour, cake flour,
    baking soda, baking powder, and salt and set aside.

3. In another bowl, combine the butter, oil, and sugar. Add the eggs, almond
    extract, and honey.

4. Add the yogurt to the honey mixture, then add half of the milk.

5. Sift in half of the dry ingredients into the wet ingredients and mix well. Add the
    other half of the milk and the remainder of the dry ingredients and mix well for
    about 1 minute until batter is slightly thick.

6. Divide the batter into the prepared 4-inch molds and 4 (6-inch) pans equally.
    Bake the 6-inch rounds for 20 minutes, then bring down to 325°F and bake for
    10 to 15 more minutes, or until a toothpick inserted into the center comes out
    clean. The 4-inch mold only needs to bake for 12 to 15 minutes.

7. When the cakes have cooled and you are able to handle them, level/tort, brush
    with the simple syrup, and wrap them in plastic wrap so that you can freeze
    them for at least 1 hour.

8. In the meantime, make the buttercream: Cream the butter on medium for a
    few minutes, until light and fluffy. Add in the sifted confectioners' sugar slowly,
    followed by the almond extract and salt. Beat on medium speed for about
    2 minutes, adding the heavy cream toward the end.

9. Fill and stack the 4-inch rounds. You may pipe the buttercream on or use a spatula; use whatever you are comfortable with.

10. Crumb coat the cake and chill for 20 minutes.

11. Fill and stack the 6-inch rounds. Remember to scrape each layer as you stack, so that you can keep the cake as straight as possible.

12. Crumb coat and chill in the refrigerator for 30 minutes.

13. To make the buttercream for decorating: Color one-quarter of the Swiss meringue buttercream a soft yellow.

14. Apply your yellow frosting to the bottom third of the chilled cake.

15. Color half of the remaining three-quarters of the Swiss meringue buttercream with the excess of the first batch of yellow. Cover the middle of the cake with this color. Use the remaining uncolored buttercream to frost the rest of the cake. Frost the 4-inch tier with the white buttercream. Freeze the 4-inch for 30 minutes. Using a large spatula, smooth down the buttercream by rotating the turntable and running the palette along the cake. Then, scrape a few times with the tall scraper.

16. After a few passes with the scraper, patch any holes or crevices in the buttercream. Make sure you use the appropriate colors.

17. Scrape smooth until you are satisfied with the final coat of buttercream. You may need to take another trip to the refrigerator and do more patchwork to achieve a nice coat.

18. Cut the uneven top edges of the cake off with a sharp and wet knife. You should have a nice ombre shade on the larger tier. The small tier will be white.

CONTINUED >

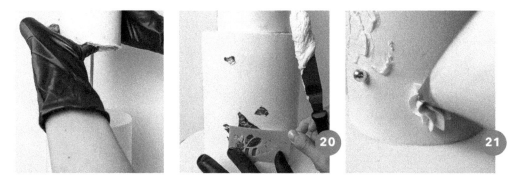

19. Push a 12-inch dowel into the center of the cake. Remove the 4-inch tier from the board. Since it has had time to freeze, it should be easy to handle wearing gloves. Center it over the dowel and push it down.

20. Place some gold leaf randomly onto the cake. Use a small palette knife to apply buttercream over the bee stencil, scrape it off with a cake scraper, and peel to reveal a thin layer of stenciled buttercream.

21. Fill a piping bag fitted with the large star tip with any excess buttercream and pipe rosettes and stars (minimal) on the cake. Remember to step back and look at the cake during the decorating process. Sometimes less is more, and you can create an effectively beautiful cake with very little effort.

22. To prepare the flowers, start by cutting a floral wire in half. Trim the flower at the top of the step near the base of the bud.

23. Insert a wire through the bottom of the bud and pull it halfway down. Hold the base of the bud and twist the wires around each other so that it creates a faux stem.

24. Take 8 inches of floral tape and wrap the wire starting at the base and working your way down. Make sure it is tight; floral tape usually has a gum paste that sticks to itself well.

25. Repeat steps 22 through 24 for however many flowers you want to add to the cake. I use about 5 or 6 flowers.

26. To make the bees, prepare the rolling pin, X-Acto knife, and 2 floral wires cut into thirds, and divide the fondant into 1-ounce and ¼-ounce portions. Color the larger portion yellow and the smaller one black.

27. Divide the yellow portion of fondant in half and roll it out to ¹⁄₁₆-inch thick (use the ¹⁄₁₆ rings on the fondant rolling pin as a guide).

28. Roll out the black fondant to the same thickness. Use the X-Acto knife to cut both the yellow and black fondant into strips about ⅛-inch wide.

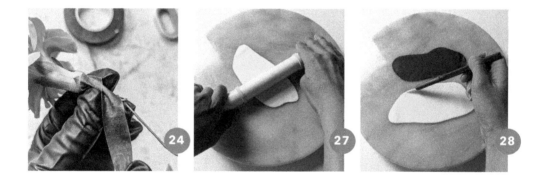

CONTINUED >

29. Alternate the strips of yellow and black to form a bee pattern.

30. Roll the fondant slightly, not too hard but just enough to merge the fondant together. You should have a flat piece of striped fondant. Trim off the ends so that they are neat and straight.

31. Cut the fondant lengthwise into thirds. Then, Cut the thirds in half; you should have 6 pieces.

32. Divide the rest of the yellow fondant into 6 pieces and roll into an oval shape. Brush some water over the body.

33. Wrap the body with the striped piece. Press firmly around the edges so that they don't come apart.

34. Fold the wafer paper in half and cut out half a heart shape with scissors.

35. Stick the paper wing on the back of the bee. You may use edible glue or a tiny amount of water to make it stick.

36. Hook a wire under the bee. The fondant will have to dry for 1 or 2 days.

37. Push a bundle of flowers into a jumbo straw and insert it into the top of the cake. Place the bees randomly among the flowers and cake.

Give the bees personality by drawing cute little eyes on them!

AISLE BE THERE FOR YOU

EQUIPMENT NEEDED

1 (8-cavity) silicone 4-inch cake mold

4 (6-inch) round cake pans

6 (9-inch) round cake pans

Cake board/drum

Turntable

Palette knives

Tall cake scraper

12-inch food-safe wooden dowel

Jumbo/bubble tea straws

Flowers of various sizes

Scissors

Floral wire (24 or 26 gauge)

Filler plants, such as eucalyptus, baby's breath, waxflower, and Queen Anne's lace

Floral tape

PREP TIME 1 hour

BAKE TIME 1 hour 15 minutes

DECORATING TIME 2 hours

MAKES 1 (3-tiered) cake (9-inch, 6-inch, 4-inch rounds)

SERVES 20 to 25

A beautiful cascade of florals stands out against this three-tiered red velvet beauty. The fuchsia and light pink roses paired with the delicate chamomile give off a wonderfully enchanting vibe. This cake is entirely customizable for different cake and buttercream flavors. My goal is to walk you through the step of creating a three-tiered cake that is suitable for any special occasion. Depending on the number of layers you bake, the cake will be unique as far as tier heights and width go. If you feel comfortable using a different recipe, feel free to do so. For the purposes of this tutorial, I chose the red velvet as it gave me the appropriate amounts that I needed for the pans listed in the equipment section.

FOR THE CAKE

3 recipes Red Velvet Cake (page 83), doubling the amount of cream cheese filling in the red velvet recipe

Simple syrup (pages 12–13)

FOR THE BUTTERCREAM

4½ cups (9 sticks) salted butter, at room temperature

10½ cups confectioners' sugar, sifted

3 teaspoons vanilla extract

1 to 2 tablespoons heavy (whipping) cream

½ teaspoon salt

Whitener (food-safe titanium dioxide)

CONTINUED >

1. Prepare the red velvet cake. You will need to bake in batches, and the layer products should be: 8 (4-inch) rounds, 4 (6-inch) rounds, and 6 (9-inch) rounds. For the 4-inch rounds, they only need to bake at 350°F for 10 to 12 minutes.

2. Prepare the layers for stacking by leveling, brushing with the simple syrup, wrapping in plastic wrap, and freezing for 2 to 3 hours.

3. Make the cream cheese frosting to fill the cakes by doubling the recipe for it (page 83).

4. Fill and stack the 9-inch layers with the cream cheese frosting. You will want to place it on the cake board right off the bat. Crumb coat as usual and set in the refrigerator for 1 hour.

5. Frost the 9-inch round tier and cut off the edges with a sharp, wet knife. Put the cake back in the refrigerator.

6. Fill and stack the 6-inch layers. Crumb coat and chill in the refrigerator for 30 minutes.

7. Frost the 6-inch round tier and cut off the edges as you did with the larger tier. Put the cake in the refrigerator with the larger tier. Then, Fill and stack the 4-inch rounds, and crumb coat.

The straws will act as a barrier between the cake and the wrapped florals. Feel free to place them anywhere you think flowers would look nice on the cake.

8. Stick a jumbo straw in the center of the 4-inch tier and stick it all the way through so that it touches the bottom. Pull the straw out slightly at the top and trim it so that it is flush when you push it back it back in. You will be covering the straw with the final coat of buttercream. Put the cake back in the refrigerator. You should have three neatly iced, sharp-edged tiers.

9. Stick the 12-inch dowel straight down the center of the largest tier.

10. Depending on how many flowers you are using, cut 6 to 12 jumbo straws into 2-inch pieces. Cut the tips so that they are slanted and pointy, so they are easier to stick into the cake. Place them into the medium tier, cascading down like a spiral. Gently push the straws into the cake so that only the holes are visible.

11. Repeat steps 12 with the largest tier. Place the large tier in the refrigerator and the medium one in the freezer.

12. Prepare the florals. Begin by cutting a piece of the floral wire in half. Cut the stem of a flower right below the base of the bud.

13. Take the wire and thread it through the stem portion of the flower. Pull it down so that it is half the length of what you started with. Start twisting the end of the wire and follow the twist up the entire length of the wire. You should have a twisted wire in lieu of an actual stem to support the rose.

14. Repeat steps 12 and 13 with the other flowers, except for filler plants that cannot be cut so easily. Now you can prepare to bunch them.

15. Grab some fillers and pair them with the flowers. Use the floral tape to wrap the entire bunch so that it has one big stem.

CONTINUED >

16. Create more bunches with the rest of the florals. You should have roughly 10 to 14 bunches depending on how many you want on the cake. Let them sit at room temperature. A friendly word of advice: avoid putting florals in the freezer. They can only withstand temperatures around 33°F to 37°F.

Keep in mind where the front of the cake is and keep everything consistent as far as how you want the front to be presented.

17. When the medium tier has been in the freezer for at least 1 hour, cut it off the board where you frosted it and handle with gloves to place on top of the large tier, centered on the dowel. Let it slide down onto the dowel.

18. Place the flower bundles in the jumbo straws that have been placed in the cake. I chose to do a diagonal cascade, as seen in the photo at the beginning of this tutorial.

19. If you have extra flowers, place wires in them and wrap with floral tape, then stick the flowers into the areas around the bundles that need to be filled. The best thing to do is to step away from the cake so that you can see what needs to be touched up.

For me, decorating started with cupcakes. I discovered that I loved piping rosettes and stars, and over time I developed a signature style to pair with unique color palettes.

I always make sure I make extra batter when baking cake layers just so I can bake cupcakes and have them lying around to decorate for fun.

CUPCAKES & CAKE POPS

RAINBOWS AND CLOUDS RED VELVET CUPCAKES

EQUIPMENT NEEDED
5 (4-by-12-inch or bigger) piping bags
1 E and round (12 or equivalent)
 piping tips
Plastic wrap
1–2 tsp nonpareils
Food coloring (5 to 7 colors of choice)

PREP TIME 30 minutes
BAKE TIME 20 to 25 minutes
DECORATING TIME 10 minutes
MAKES 1 dozen regular-size cupcakes

Red velvet cupcakes get a beautiful rainbow swirl and a dash of nonpareils. A round tip helps pipe fluffy buttercream clouds. The rainbow does not have to be a traditional one: Be creative with your colors!

½ recipe Red Velvet Cake (page 83); yields 12 to 14 cupcakes

½ recipe Vanilla Buttercream (page 28)

1. Prepare all of the ingredients listed above and have them ready in bowls and on trays.

2. Divide the buttercream into 5 to 7 bowls, color them each a different color, and put them separately into uncut piping bags. The bags should only be filled a little over halfway and all ends untrimmed. Be sure to leave ¼-cup portion white for the clouds.

3. Lay down a piece of plastic wrap. Cut one of the bags and pipe the first color of the rainbow palette in a line onto the plastic wrap. Pipe the next color of the rainbow and continue with the other colors in this fashion.

4. Grab the ends of the plastic wrap and roll the frosting up into a tube shape.

CONTINUED >

5. Cut off the excess of only one end of the frosting tube.

6. Trim a piping bag to fit the shape of a large piping nozzle (in this case I used a 1E). Fit the bag into a tall glass. Stick the cut end of the tube of frosting straight down into the bag.

7. Holding the bag comfortably and with a tight enough grip, center the tip over the cupcake. Use a gentle squeeze and pipe a swirl on the cupcake in one motion, starting from the center.

8. Use a medium round tip like a 12 to pipe dots like puffy clouds.

9. Use a spoon or clean fingers to sprinkle on nonpareils. Decorate the remaining cupcakes in the same manner.

You can also add a dash of edible glitter to make the rainbow pop.

FLORAL LUXE CUPCAKES

EQUIPMENT NEEDED
3 1M (large star), 8B (open star), 4B,
  and 224 (drop flower) piping tips
6 (4-by-12-inch or bigger) piping tips
Gel food coloring (5 to 7 drops for
  each bold color, 2 to 4 drops for each
  pastel color used)

PREP TIME 30 minutes
BAKE TIME 20 to 25 minutes
DECORATING TIME 20 minutes
MAKES 1 dozen regular-size cupcakes

A classic, warm vanilla sponge is embellished with a floral piping flourish. Pastels in white, navy, grey, pink, and teal take over this palette. You will learn two designs so that the cupcakes show variety.

½ recipe From-Scratch Vanilla Cake
(page 14); you should be able to
bake 12 to 14 cupcakes

½ recipe Vanilla Buttercream (page 28)
Sprinkles of your choice

1. Divide the buttercream into 3 large parts and 3 smaller ones. Reserve the large parts for the 1M tips. Color each part to your liking. Refer to the equipment list for the number of drops required to make pastels and bolds.

2. Fill the bags and pair tips as you prefer.

3. Using one of the 1M bags, hold the tip straight above the cupcake and pipe a shape like a question mark. You should be left with what looks like half of a heart on the upper left corner of the cupcake.

CONTINUED >

4. Use another 1M color to pipe the same shape slightly over the first one. This shape should cover only a small portion. Use the 8B to pipe a large star.

5. Use the 4B tip to pipe a few stars in the empty spaces. Then, Fill in the extra spaces with the 224-(drop flower) tip.

6. Finish off by using sprinkles of your choice, the smaller the better.

7. For the second design, start by using the third 1M color. Pipe the left side of a heart shape. Then, Use a different color of 1M to pipe the other half of the heart.

8. Use the 8B to pipe a large star at the bottom tip of the heart. Pipe some 4B star accents. Use a 1M color to pipe a star accent to the bottom left.

9. Fill in the extra spaces with the 224-(drop flower) tip.

10. Finish with sprinkles. Continue decoarting the cupcakes, alternating the decorating style.

HEARTS OF GOLD

EQUIPMENT NEEDED
Small and medium flat brushes
Oil-based food coloring
Silicone heart gem mold (8-cavity)
Small baking tray
1 small piping bag

PREP TIME 1 hour 30 minutes
DECORATING TIME 20 minutes
MAKES 8 cake heart gems

Of all the pretty cake treats out there, I have a soft spot for heart gems. The geometric lines give off a modern, fun look while housing delicious cake flavors. The best part about making gems is filling them with a flavor of your choice, *and* you can use cake trimmings or layers leftover from making a cake. In this tutorial you will learn how to use oil-based coloring on white chocolate and an easy method for filling the hearts. The molds can be found online through many retailers.

½ cup buttercream of choice
3 cups cubed cake leftovers
1 (12-ounce) package candy melts
Edible gold leaf sheets

Nonpareils or sprinkles (optional)
Fondant decorations using any molds
   of choice (see Beachy Cakesicles,
   page 161, for instructions)

1. Make sure the buttercream is at room temperature before mixing.

2. To make the filling: Add half the buttercream to the bowl of cake cubes. Wearing gloves, mix the filling together by hand. You may add more buttercream if the filling does not hold shape when you mold it into a ball.

3. Microwave the candy melts for 15 to 30 seconds at a time. Stir the candy melts until they are smooth with no solid bits.

4. Spoon 1 tablespoon of candy melts into the cavity. If you have an 8-cavity mold, make 4 in the same color.

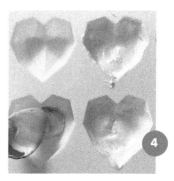

CONTINUED >

5. Use a flat brush to spread the candy melts in the mold up the sides, trying not to go over the edges.

6. In a separate bowl, use oil-based coloring to make 1 tablespoon of candy melts a different color of your choice. Mix well and try not to overmix.

7. In the same container you heated the melts in, add a bit of darker coloring. Swirl this color, but do not mix. A few stirs should do.

8. Add the color from the smaller bowl into the swirled color. Stir gently to achieve a more apparent swirl of the two colors.

9. Spoon this mixture into 2 cavities as you did before.

10. Use a flat brush to spread the mixture up the sides and make sure the bottom is covered.

11. Now completely mix the swirled melts so that it becomes one color. Repeat the same process of filling the remaining cavities with this color.

12. Take the cake filling mixture and make a ball about the size of 2 tablespoons. Push the ball into one cavity and spread it evenly with your finger. Make sure there is some space above the filling so that it does not reach the edges.

13. Continue with the rest of the cake and cavities. Chill in the refrigerator for 30 minutes.

14. After they have chilled, reheat the leftover candy melts and fill the top of the hearts with a couple of teaspoons of the melts. Use a palette knife to spread the mixture down and scrape the edges clean. Freeze for 1 hour. When the hearts are ready, you will be able to peel them out of the mold easily.

15. Arrange them with some space in between on a baking tray lined with parchment paper. Place the gold leaf sheets on two of the hearts.

16. Use a medium flat brush to gently smooth the gold leaf onto the hearts.

17. Reheat the remainder of the melts and put them in a small uncut piping bag. Cut a very small part of the tip off.

18. Drizzle over two of the white gems. While the drizzle is still melted, add the nonpareils or sprinkles (if using).

19. Pipe a small bit of candy melts onto the two solid color gems.

20. Place the prepared fondant decorations onto the melts so they stick.

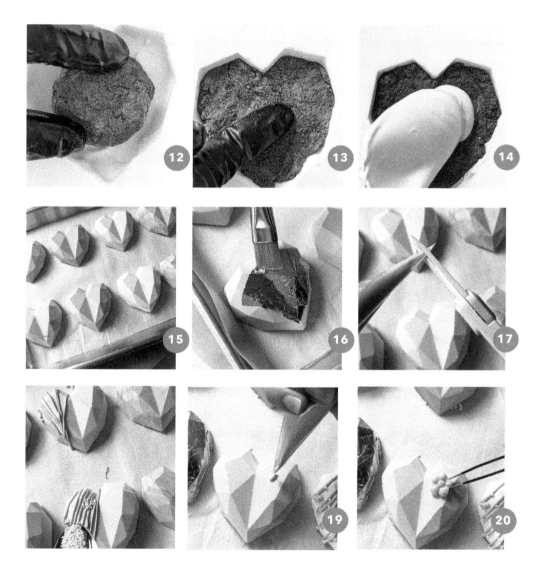

STRAWBERRY LEMONADE CUPCAKES

EQUIPMENT NEEDED
Pink gel food coloring (optional)
1 large piping bag
1M piping tip
Paper straws
Oven-friendly paper cups

PREP TIME 15 minutes
BAKE TIME 15 to 20 minutes
DECORATING TIME 10 minutes
MAKES 1 dozen cupcakes

A lemony sponge cake is topped with a tall swirl of strawberry buttercream to make these fun cupcakes. A brightly colored paper straw and slice of fresh lemon placed on top give these a refreshing look. These use oven-friendly liners for a tall look. You can find them in most cake supply stores or online.

- -

FOR THE STRAWBERRY BUTTERCREAM
2 cups (4 sticks) salted butter, at room
  temperature
5 cups confectioners' sugar, sifted

4 tablespoons freeze-dried strawberry
  powder (use 1 [1-ounce] package of
  freeze-dried strawberries and a food
  processor to make the powder)

FOR THE CUPCAKES
1 or 2 lemons
3 tablespoons granulated sugar
½ recipe Mini Lemon and Olive Oil
  Cakes (page 71)

2 to 4 tablespoons colorful
  sprinkle medley

- -

1. Make the strawberry buttercream: Cream the butter on medium speed until light and fluffy. Slowly add the confectioners' sugar. When it is smooth, add the strawberry powder and stir until well incorporated.

2. If you want to make the color of the buttercream pop, add a few drops of pink food coloring.

3. Fit the 1M tip into the large bag and fill it with the strawberry buttercream.

4. Cut a paper straw into thirds. You should only need 4 straws.

5. Cut a lemon in half and make 12 slices. Place a lemon slice in a bowl with the granulated sugar. Flip over the lemon so that the other side is sugared as well.

CONTINUED >

6. Start a swirl with the piping bag in the center of the cupcake and go around the edges. Continue to build the swirl until you are satisfied with the height.

7. Finish by lifting the tip off the top to make a little peak.

8. Place a tiny straw in the swirl, a little offset. Place a sugared lemon slice on the swirl next to the straw.

If you do not plan on serving the cupcakes right away, use lemon jelly slices instead.

9. Use a spoon to add sprinkles. Continue to decorate the rest of the cupcakes.

BEACHY CAKESICLES

EQUIPMENT NEEDED
Oil-based food coloring (2 drops of
  each color used, 2 to 3 colors)
4-cavity cakesicle mold
Small or medium flat brushes
Small cakesicle sticks (similar to ice
  pop sticks but smaller)

Palette knife
Fondant Seashell fondant mold
Fondant roller
Small cake scraper
PREP TIME 15 minutes
DECORATING TIME 1 hour 30 minutes
MAKES 4 cakesicles

These fun cakesicles are for the ocean lovers out there. You can use up leftover cake
or bake a small cake to create a new delicious and playful treat. Cake supply retailers
offer a wide variety of cakesicle molds. This tutorial will take you through the steps of
creating a basic one that yields an impressive result, nonetheless. We will be coloring
bright white candy melts to achieve the beautiful oceanic swirls. If you do not have
any oil-based colorings, you may use colored melts to achieve a similar effect.

2 cups cake (trimmings or leftovers)
  cut into large cubes
¼ cup buttercream of choice
1 (12-ounce) package candy
  melts, melted

Fondant
¼ teaspoon cornstarch
2 to 3 tablespoons crushed graham
  crackers

1. Prepare the cake filling the same way as the Hearts of Gold (page 153).

2. Separate the candy melts so you have two small portions and one larger one.

3. Use two different colors (a light blue and a dark blue) in one large and one small
    portion. Swirl the colors, but do not mix completely.

4. Add the smaller portion of swirled color into the larger, unmixed portion. Swirl
    the two together but do not mix completely.

5. Dip a medium flat brush into the swirled mixture and coat each cavities of
    the mold.

6. Tap the mold on a flat surface gently to smooth out the melts. Chill in the refrig-
    erator for 20 minutes.

CONTINUED >

7. After the melts have set, fill the cavities with the cake-and-buttercream mix. Try not to overfill so you have room to pour more melts.

8. Insert a cakesicle stick into the slot near the handle of the mold.

9. Use a greased palette knife to pat down the cake fillings.

10. Reheat the candy melts you colored and spoon a small portion onto the filling.

11. Use a palette knife to spread it evenly and remove excess from the edges. Freeze for 1 hour or leave overnight in the refrigerator.

12. For the decorations, prepare fondant the size of a golf ball. Add the cornstarch to rid of any stickiness. Push small portions of the fondant into each cavity in the mold. Use a fondant roller to press the fondant further into the mold.

13. Using the edge of the scraper, press and drag firmly over the shape to trim off excess fondant.

14. Gently peel the shapes out of the mold. You should have a nice assortment of seashell shapes.

15. When they are ready, gently pop the cakesicles with sticks out of the mold.

16. Reheat the small portion of uncolored candy melts and use a flat brush to make a foamy appearance on the cakesicles.

17. While the melts are still wet, add some graham-cracker sand to the base of each cakesicle. Brush on more of the white melts to continue the wavy, foamy look.

18. Dab a small amount of melts onto the back of the fondant decorations. Stick the fondant decorations to the cakesicles.

UNICORN CAKE JARS

EQUIPMENT NEEDED
2 piping bags
2 1M piping tips
Fondant roller
Small heart cookie cutter
Small brush

PREP TIME 20 minutes
BAKE TIME 30 to 35 minutes
DECORATING TIME 15 minutes
MAKES 3 (16-ounce) jars

For this recipe, you'll cut up the cake into large cubes to layer in a jar with frosting. Go the extra mile by making the jars into unicorns, perfect for any colorful party. Make the horn and ears the day before, so that they have time to harden. The eyelashes can be applied to the jar in a soft state.

½ recipe Sprinkle Party Cake (page 87)
½ recipe Vanilla Buttercream
  (page 28), divided into 3 parts and
  colored 3 different colors
Sprinkles

1 golf ball–size ball black fondant
1 baseball–size ball white fondant
1 teaspoon vodka or equivalent
  hard alcohol
Gold highlighter dust

1. Begin by cutting the cake into 1-inch cubes and put them in a bowl.

2. Place the cubes of cake into one of the jars to make a layer, spreading quite evenly. Use a spoon to gently level the cake a bit.

3. Use the first bag of colored buttercream fitted with the 1M tip to swirl a layer of buttercream frosting into the jar. Make sure you cover the cake by swirling over the middle, too. Place a second layer of cake on top of the layer of buttercream.

CONTINUED >

4. Use the second 1M tip and colored buttercream to swirl another layer over the cake. Place a final layer of cake on top.

5. Make a fluffy swirl on top with the last color of buttercream. Add sprinkles; be generous!

6. Prepare the fondants on a clean surface. Roll the black fondant into a skinny log shape. Cut the log into thirds. Cut the thirds into halves. You should have 6 pieces.

7. Take one piece and cut a third off. Cut that third into half and toss (or save) one half. You will not need it.

8. You should be left with one bigger and one small piece. Shape the bigger piece into an eye line. Take the smaller piece to make a lash and stick it at the tail end of the eye.

9. Do the same with the other 5 pieces of fondant until you have 3 pairs of eyes with lashes.

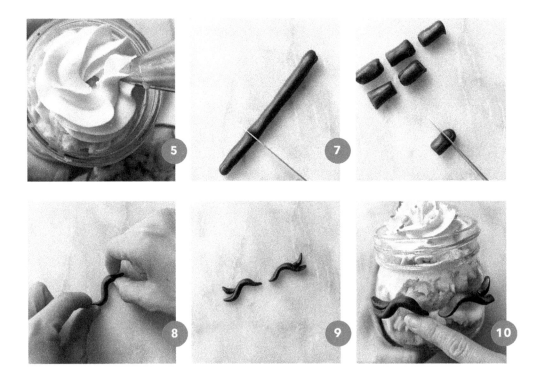

10. While they are soft, stick them onto the jars, two on each. Then chill the jars in the refrigerator for an hour.

11. Roll the white fondant to a ¼-inch thickness. And Cut out 6 small hearts with the cookie cutter.

12. Pinch the top of a heart with one hand and shape the pointed end from behind so it takes the form of an ear. Make 6 ears and set them aside.

13. Take the remainder of the fondant and cut it into thirds. Cut a third in half. And Shape the two halves into a tube with a narrow ends. Starting with the wider end, twist the tubes around each other gently. Gently hold the narrow end and twist at the wide end so that the fondant does not tear. Pinch the narrow end slightly to close the horn.

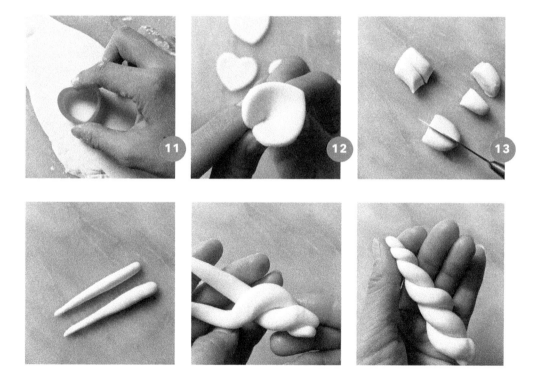

CONTINUED >

14. Insert a toothpick at the base of the horn so that half is sticking out. Stick the ears onto the buttercream. Stick the horn on top behind the ears.

15. Mix the alcohol with ½ teaspoon of gold highlighter dust.

16. Paint the horn. If you need more highlighter dust, feel free to add it to the alcohol mixture. Finish decorating the rest of the jars in the same manner.